# My Yoke Is Easy, My Burden Light

*Also by Mary M. Varick:*

*Not Without Tears*
*Till Death . . .*

# My Yoke Is Easy, My Burden Light

## Mary M. Varick

**magnificat press**

Avon, NJ

My Yoke Is Easy, My Burden Light
Copyright 1960 Mary M. Varick
All rights reserved
ISBN 0-940543-25-7
Library of Congress catalog number 90-063355
Printed in the USA


Magnificat Press
315 Main St.
Avon, NJ 07717
Previously published (1960) by Our Lady of the Cape
Publications, Cap-de-la-Madeleine, Quebec, Canada

THE SECRETARY OF STATE,
VATICAN CITY.

*Vatican City,*
*June 11, 1960.*

*First Saturday Club,*
*Mrs. Mary M. Varick,*
*241 Pacific Ave.,*
*Jersey City, N.J., U.S.A.*

*The Secretary of State of His Holiness is directed by the Holy Father to acknowledge receipt of the loyal address presented to Him on the behalf of the First Saturday Club, to assure the officers and members of His prayers for the success of their efforts in organizing pilgrimages in favor of the handicapped and to convey to them and all who assist, in pledge of richest heavenly graces and divine favors, His cordial, paternal Apostolic Blessing.*

Seal of the
Secretariat of State
of His Holiness.

# In Memoriam

This book is dedicated to the members of our family who have died since the publication of Mom's third book, Till Death . . . They are her brothers Joseph Cassidy and Fr. John Cassidy; a nephew, Jimmy Cassidy, and a sister-in-law, Helen Cassidy (the son and the wife of Mom's late brother James Cassidy). We find comfort and hope in the words of Jesus: "I am the resurrection and the life; whoever believes in me, even if he dies, will live, and everyone who lives and believes in me will never die."

Mary Pisaniello
Easton, Pennsylvania
July 26, 1990
Feast of St. Anne

# Contents

# Foreword

Dear Reader:

Congratulations!
Yes, may I congratulate you on opening this book to read! Because in our everyday life we do many things that have almost no moral bearings, that seem to be neither good nor bad. Some, let's face it, are not good at all! But in picking up this book with the intention of reading it you are undertaking an action that will influence your life, that may have a bearing on your eternity!

Why?

Well, in everyday life we meet so many people who just "exist," but the deep meaning of their life seems to escape them. They live superficially, indifferently. God is far away. Whatever influence He may have in their daily routine is reduced to a minimum.

The biography you are about to read is different. Mary Varick, still young, heard her mother tell her that God in heaven was her Father. And you know what? She believed it. And she lived accordingly, speaking with Him, telling Him about her dreams (that a teenager in a wheelchair could have dates, hope to marry, raise children . . .), asking His advice and following her Father's voice, keeping Him in her joys and sorrows.

And do you know what? Because Mary Varick is a child to God, God is a Father to Mary Varick, not only in words but in reality!

Mary Varick reminds us of a modern Job. You do remember

Job's story in the Holy Scriptures, don't you?

He seemed to have everything to make life enjoyable. And Satan's reaction to God: "It is easy for him to serve You. He has everything. But test him. Put forth Your hand and touch him, and You shall see." Job lost his money, his properties, his house, but persisted in praising God. Satan still protested before God: "But he has not been touched in his bone and his flesh." And the Almighty permitted that Job be tried in his body. Sickness overcame him.

And yet the same praises came forth from his lips: The Lord gave, and the Lord hath taken away. Blessed be the name of the Lord."

Divine Providence apparently took Mary Varick through somewhat the same road. He took away from her the little money she had, her property, her house, some of her friends. But her love seemed indefectible. So she was ready for the great test. Doctors told her she would not live more than a few months. Her reaction to someone who enquired if she was afraid of death? "It will be just like meeting an old friend face to face after you have been carrying on telephone conversations for so many years." That sentence reveals what kind of person Mary Varick is.

One would think that all these afflictions would hamper her life. Yet she is one of the most cheerful persons you could meet, dearly loved by all who come in contact with her, and deeply cherished by her husband and children.

Here is Mary Varick's own story. Her first words are now almost true: "It is, indeed, a strange feeling to know that by the time anyone ever gets to read this manuscript I will be blind." But in her heart burns a fire of love for the Sacred Heart that few well people have ever obtained. Mary herself might never have known such great love had she not been chosen to be a member of God's "inner circle," as she calls those who are handicapped.

Reader , may you also understand, and may the love of God that burns in her heart also burn in yours when you finish reading this book.

Father Jacques Rinfret, OMI
Pilgrimage Director at
Our Lady of the Cape,
Canada' s National Shrine to Mary

# Introduction

## Fr. Paul Bochicchio

From the first time I met Mary Varick close to twenty-three years ago I sensed very strongly her love and understanding of youth. At that time I was a seminarian working in St. Lucy's parish in Newark, N.J. Mary often attended Mass there since she lived a short distance away at the Colonade Apartments in Newark; I suggested that St. Lucy's might be a good place for a First Saturday Club Mass. I felt that our schoolchildren and teenagers would have an excellent opportunity to use their talents to help others, and so the First Saturday Club descended upon St. Lucy's—the first of a number of significant visits that many years later would include Mary's wedding to Jerry Sheehan on October 3, 1981, and the celebration of her funeral Mass on July 1, 1989 (both First Saturdays, I might add!).

Mary not only enjoyed the presence of young people; she actually had a way of "being young" with them, something that I think all of us began to realize as she approached that moment of being "eternally young" with the Lord. She did so with the excitement of a child setting out on a new adventure. After my ordination to the priesthood in May, 1971, I was sent to Our Lady of Mercy parish in Jersey City. I became involved with a ministry of the young people of the parish called The

Seekers—the name "Seekers" came from a young man who returned from our first youth retreat in 1971 and stated, as our first "little flock" gathered around the tabernacle for prayer, that we should be known as The Seekers since we would spend our lives seeking to know Jesus.

As our Seeker movement began to grow I began giving some thought to how I might help them to experience Jesus on an ongoing basis. The retreats were a great beginning, but as we often reflected at the close of each retreat, we needed to return to "the valley" and the reality of our day-to-day lives, and could not remain "on the mountain." The Gospel account of the Transfiguration became for us the Scriptural reflection that often aided us in our transition from the retreat house in the country to the reality of city life. In effect, I was looking for an apostolate that would be an ongoing experience for our Seekers. The follow-up to our retreats centered around meetings held every Sunday night, when we would discuss the tensions, joys and struggles of the week in the manner of a Cursillo group reunion and end with shared prayer. We also had monthly Masses. We began to become involved in some ways in the parish, with senior citizen/seeker parties, helping out at the parish feast and carnival, but there was a need for something more.

In July, 1973, nearly two years after our Seeker group had come into being, Mary Varick spoke to them and won their hearts, and we soon embarked on our first Canadian pilgrimage with the First Saturday Club. Some of The Seekers went by plane and the rest of us went by car. Mary was enthusiastic about the idea and very supportive of this young priest and his Seekers. Anyone who knew Mary quickly knew that Murphy's Law and all its attendant corollaries were a way of life for her

First Saturday family. The involvement of The Seekers was certainly no exception to this rule. Kids were kids, and they certainly acted like kids—pilgrimage or no pilgrimage, much to the bewilderment of their priest-moderator, who probably expected them to be more like saints than like The Seekers.

On that first pilgrimage they pulled a number of stunts (for the most part harmless), such as the wheelchair races down the ramps of Madonna House at Cap-de-la-Madeleine, leaving tire skid marks on the new indoor-outdoor carpets. (At a recent visit to Madonna House I noticed that the ramps had been dismantled—I wonder why?) They sped in a car through the small town of Beaupre at sixty miles per hour, bought Sangria wine (which I managed to confiscate), etc. You might say that The Seekers were seeking in all the wrong directions, but at the same time they worked hard and cared for the handicapped, and when they prayed and shared with the group, they really touched the First Saturday Club. In exchange, they were really touched by what they experienced in the faith, the joyful acceptance of crosses, the laughter and the undeniable joy of Ann Gerhardt and Lucy Gangi, and the playful antics of Ron Pewsie and Howie Daniels.

Though yours truly probably started to turn prematurely gray at age twenty-eight, Mary Varick took it all in stride. She believed in kids, but not in a naive fashion, because she was also painfully aware of what they were up against, and of how many forces in our society were really drawing them away from Jesus. Mary affirmed me and strongly supported my work with these kids—she was so touched by their openness to Jesus.

Toward the end of that first pilgrimage we attended I discovered that the First Saturday Club had been banned from the Auberge guest house at St. Anne's Basilica (a facility designed for the convenience of the disabled and handicapped) because of the antics and (in some cases destructive) exploits of the young people. For several years after that pilgrimage, the group had to stay at motels far down the road from the basilica that were certainly not designed to handle the needs of handicapped and disabled people. For all that, Mary still believed enough in the kids and in their goodness to embrace The Seekers with open arms despite what involvement with them had cost the First Saturday Club.

In so many ways, from that day on The Seekers and the First Saturday Club formed an unbreakable bond. My dream of having an apostolate for our kids, and the First Saturday Club's need for young, strong and caring volunteers proved to be an answer to mutual prayer.

On December 7, 1974, the First Saturday Club came to Our Lady of Mercy for the first time for their monthly First Saturday Mass. The Seekers were there, as they were for so many of the monthly Masses and luncheons in other parishes—assisting with wheelchairs, waiting on tables, entertaining, praying with their new extended family, basking always in the warmth of Mary's gratitude and affirmation, which helped them in their struggle for self-esteem and self-worth.

Just over two years later , at the First Saturday Mass at Our Lady of Mercy on New Year's Day, 1977, Mary announced that there would be a pilgrimage to Russia, Rome, Assisi and Lourdes that very summer. With the efforts and generosity of The Seekers and the other societies of Our Lady of Mercy parish, we presented Mary with the first $1,000 toward the trip. Later that year, among the sixty or so members of the pilgrimage were a number of Seekers, who witnessed the Church behind the Iron Curtain, prayed the rosary in Russia, celebrated the Eucharist in the presence of communist young adults who had to attend Mass because they had to be with us wherever we went) and witnessed to those young adults. Our Seekers were motivated enough by the love of Jesus to raise their own money and spend their energy and time to care for the disabled members of the First Saturday Club. Somehow or other, I believe, Mary's vision, her insistence on having the young people on the pilgrimage, her great leap in faith that added much to her suffering and financial indebtedness—and yet, like all great works of God, inspired by the Spirit—added to the state of life and the renewal of faith in Russia.

While in Rome, The Seekers presented Mary with a beautiful wall plaque of Our Lady of Mercy; shortly afterwards, she presented The Seekers with a large framed copy of "The Comforter," a beautiful painting of Jesus with His arm around a teenage boy. It was later proudly mounted on the wall of The Seekers' room in the school basement at Our Lady of Mercy, and now hangs on the wall of the parish meeting room.

In January 1983 I left Our Lady of Mercy and The Seekers and Junior Seekers (elementary school members) after eleven and a half years, during which five hundred young people had made retreats and a number of them had their faith in Jesus strengthened through the touch of the First Saturday Club. As I began my work as campus minister and religion teacher at Roselle Catholic High School, I again turned to Mary to help me open the door a little wider to Christ for the young people I wanted to serve. Again Mary touched hearts when she spoke to my religion classes and campus ministry group, and the following year several young people from Roselle Catholic made Seeker retreats and came on the pilgrimage to Canada. I remember one time asking Paul Russell, a young man who was a quadriplegic as the result of an accident, was a member of the First Saturday Club and had a Master's Degree in Spirituality from Fordham University, to address my junior morality class on the issue of the right to life. His faith, upbeat sense of hope and deep love for life, so characteristic of the First Saturday Club, deeply touched my students.

In February 1985 I became pastor of Holy Rosary parish in Jersey City, and as I turned my attention to the need to involve the youth of the parish I again turned to Mary Varick. She and her husband Jerry Sheehan spoke to our young people at our first CYO retreat in May 1985, and in the following July the Holy Rosary youth and the youth of Roselle Catholic embraced the First Saturday Club family.

In the summer of 1987, many of our Holy Rosary kids accompanied the First Saturday Club to Rome, Assisi and the Holy Land, walked where Jesus had walked, reflected on His life, met the Holy Father, and witnessed the example of faith offered by our disabled brothers and sisters. As one of our Seekers said, "Spending time with the First Saturday Club teaches you how handicapped you are. Isn't that what it is all about in a world of so much disunity, in a world where we so easily erect walls? Isn't it the work of the Spirit that we discover in our differences (which are only superficial after all) how much we need each other and in needing each other how we meet Christ?"

Mary's health did not permit her to attend the last pilgrimage to Rome and the Holy Land, but her spirit was certainly there, as was her heritage, especially to the young. I often think of the retreats at which she spoke, the days of recollection she helped me give, especially to our junior high students at Our Lady of Mercy. I won't forget the great honor she gave to The Seekers by making a Seeker retreat and by becoming a Seeker in much the same way that The Seekers and other young people whose lives she touched became members of the First Saturday Club.

I think of Fr. Kevin Carter, a Seeker from Our Lady of Mercy, whose vocation to the priesthood was greatly influenced by the First Saturday Club. I think of young people who now serve others, some the handicapped and disabled, because Mary Varick welcomed them into the First Saturday family. At a time when so many were impatient and critical of youth, she saw the image of Jesus in them. I think of young people who experienced no generation gap when they sat with a woman old enough to be their grandmother and confided their troubles, struggles and dreams to her and found the compassion and understanding of someone who reflected Jesus to them because she knew Him so well.

I think of Mary Varick Sheehan, who ached for the young people who were victims of a society that so often lied to them, leading them into drugs, sexual experimentation and all those things that lead away from Jesus. I think of a woman who joyfully offered her pain, in hours of simple and direct conversation with Jesus in the Blessed Sacrament, for the young especially. I think of a woman who chided priests and other adults who thought that kids were too much trouble to work with.

As I ascended the pulpit of St. Lucy's Church on July 1, 1989, to preach at Mary's funeral as I had been asked to do, I felt that the only difficult task was to limit what could be said about someone who from a wheelchair and in defiance of so many other restrictions believed in God's goodness and trusted even when there was no reasonable explanation for doing so—someone who offered her life as an act of gratitude to make what could have been a sad world a better place, especially for the generations that would follow her. As a mother, grandmother and great-grandmother she left a beautiful heritage to her family, but in the relatively short time I knew her she became a mother, grandmother and great-grandmother to many beyond her own biological family. Her joy, her faith, her laughter and her love of the "laughing Jesus," her embrace of the life to come, and her ability to see Jesus in everyone and in all of the paradoxes of life made me so grateful to God to have the opportunity to proclaim the Gospel that Mary Varick Sheehan wrote with her life.

Now let her begin her story . . .

# CHAPTER ONE

## A Love Affair

It is, indeed, a strange feeling to know that by the time any one ever gets to read this manuscript I'll be blind. Oh, I admit that in the beginning this realization brought bitter mental anguish, but in recent days I've learned to wear my own "crown of thorns" with better grace, and now I long only to share the wonder of my life with others who have not yet learned that gracious acceptance of affliction truly leads one to God's "inner circle." Since the blessings that are mine defy poor human words, I've begged the Holy Spirit to be my "ghost writer."

If I try to thank God for my blessings in the order in which I received them, my first effort would be to let Him know how grateful I am for my parents and family. No other folks in the world could have made life such a joy. And next I think I'd like to thank Him for being born in the United States. If I could only tell you how often I shuddered during the war years, when I read of the cruel, sadistic nations destroying their weak and maimed. Truly, my heart would fill with gratitude for being an American because I have been severely crippled with polio since infancy, and yet my life has been richer and fuller than the lives of people who have never known affliction.

But I guess the real story of my life begins, as all good stories do — with a love affair. As I look back, that phase of my life seems more fantastic than Cinderella, or Snow White or any of the other famous fairy tales. Who'd expect the handsome hero to fall in love with and marry a cripple? Gay, good-looking Bill, who could charm any girl in the crowd, who loved dancing and sports, first entered my life as "the boy next door" during our summer vacation the year I finished high school.

It would be nice to be able to tell you that ours was a whirlwind romance, love at first sight and all that sort of thing, but nothing would be farther from the truth. It's true that *my* heart did nip-ups every time I saw Bill, but I knew all too well that it was his innate kindness and compassion that made him stop at the porch of our bungalow for a brief visit each day. Oh, how grateful I am for God's gift of a sense of humor and the ability to laugh at myself, for I heard later on that Bill had told his friends he just couldn't walk by "that laughing, pretty girl who was crippled."

As the summer weeks went by, the brief visits became longer, and sometimes, when Bill had no special date, he'd sit on our porch the whole evening. Yes, there were times when our long talks lasted into the wee hours of the morning, and while he brought an unbelievable happiness into my life, it was rewarding to know that he, too, was deriving something from our friendship. Thanks to my wonderful mother and dad, and their deep and sincere love for God, I'd grown up with the firm conviction that those who bore the cross of affliction held a special place in God's heart, and that I could make my whole life one big act of love for Him if I wanted to. Oh, I was convinced, even then, that I lived and loved and breathed because somewhere, somehow, there was a special job that was mine alone to do, and with patience and faith, I'd find that job some day. This kind of thinking amazed Bill, who just couldn't imagine a life full of happiness without dancing or driving or tennis or golf.

How often I thought of summer's end with dread, because I was sure that when both of our families left the lake and returned to our winter homes the regular routine of Bill's life would absorb him and he'd soon forget his summer neighbor. Certainly, nothing about our long talks had been interesting enough to make him journey from his town to ours to renew them. "Be grateful for the happiness that you've known this summer," I sternly told myself, and then added wistfully, "he *might* be here again next summer."

I needn't tell you, then, of the joy I knew when Bill began to make fairly regular visits to our home during the winter months that followed. It made me so happy to know that he considered me one of his best friends, and that often he'd confide all the problems of his latest romance to me, or ask my opinion regarding his ambitions and his work. Sometimes he'd take me for a ride, and when he insisted on taking me to dinner, I can't even describe my feelings. As I hobbled along on my crutches, he treated me with all the chivalry and finesse that he might have shown the loveliest normal girl, and my heart almost burst with love and gratitude at his goodness. But even then, I was sure that I had my emotions completely under control, warning myself repeatedly that Bill's feeling for me was closer to pity than love, and that when he did finally fall in love and marry I'd go on being a friend of his who'd be truly grateful for my share of his life.

Another summer rolled around, and once again we were back at the lake. Except for the fact that we were closer friends and spent more time together, it was much the same as the summer before, and I found myself looking forward to Labor Day with the same sense of loss. After all, I saw Bill much more often in the summer than I did during the winter months, and I kept waiting for the day he'd tell me that he'd fallen in love. "Oh, God," I often prayed, "give me the grace to be glad for him, when that day comes, for a wonderful guy like that deserves a special kind of happiness."

And so I come to the moment in my life that even now, after all these years, seems incredible. I didn't see Bill for a few weeks after Labor Day, and when, at last, he called and asked me to go for a ride, the joy I felt knew no bounds. But I was totally unprepared for what he had to say, as the car moved smoothly along over country roads. "I've deliberately stayed away these weeks so that I could be sure of what I'm saying now," Bill told me. "I find life very dull without you, and it annoys me to find that most girls live in a dull little world of dates and dances and dresses. I want to marry you, Mary." As I sat in stunned silence, he went on, "I never gave a thought to God's universe until I watched the moon come up with you, and found that you knew almost every star by name. My only knowledge of the sunrise was a tired glimpse of it on the way home from a prom, until I sat on the cliff with you, and through your eyes watched the miracle of a new day begin. You've got a kind of beauty and understanding I've never known, and I want to share it with you."

It took a long time for full realization to reach me, and then we talked and argued for hours on the pros and cons of marrying a cripple. At long last, we agreed to make a fervent Novena to the Sacred Heart for guidance. If He felt that ours would be a good marriage, He'd find a way to guide us, and if marriage was not for us, we'd make our Novena with perfect faith that He'd let us understand that too. In the meantime, we agreed not to mention this serious talk of ours to any one else at all.

The nine days that followed were truly ones of mixed emotions. One moment I'd be overwhelmed with the thought of being Bill's wife. The next moment I'd be terrified at so presumptuous a thought. Each evening, Bill and I made our novena — were ever prayers so fervently said before or since? On the ninth night of our novena, Bill and I were chatting over a cup of tea at our dining room table when my mother, who'd been making the mission in our parish church, walked in. She handed me a package she was carrying, and with a half-embarrassed laugh she said, "During these last days, I've had the funniest feeling that some day soon you'll have a home of your own, and I wanted to be the first one to give you a gift for that home." When I opened the package, my heart almost stopped as I looked down at one of the most beautiful house-blessings of the Sacred Heart that I have ever seen. Bill put his arms around me, and through laughter and tears we told Mom of the novena we had just completed. I can still hear Bill's whispered "What more éloquent an answer do you want, Mary dear?" And here I am, all these years later, through sight growing painfully dim, gazing adoringly at that same beloved house-blessing in its honored place in our home.

Shortly after that, Bill and I went to talk to Father O'Brien, a beloved friend as well as one of our parish priests. "We want to be married on the feast of the Sacred Heart," we told him, and in dismay he reminded us that the feast we mentioned was on a Friday. "Isn't that a strange day for a wedding," he asked, "and won't it make plans for a reception very difficult?" We told him that we planned to dedicate all of our married life to the Sacred Heart, and that His feastday was the only day we'd consider for our wedding. "Remember the famous "let 'em eat cake, Father?" Bill asked. "Well, as far as our wedding guests are concerned, 'Let them eat fish!' " Then we went on to explain that we wanted to be married very quietly, since a marriage such as ours was bound to attract curiosity-seekers. Father was willing to go along with us to a certain extent, but remained adamant on one point: "Anyone who loves the Sacred Heart so very much will surely want to invite Him to their wedding. You *will* be married with a nuptial Mass, won't you?" I conjured up all kinds of horrible nightmares — I could see myself hobbling about the altar, maybe even falling on my face, but Father would listen to none of it. "Through all the years I've known you, I've been so proud of you, Mary," Father said, "With your head held high, you've carried your affliction like a banner of love, and on your wedding day you're coming down the aisle of your church, to be given away by your Dad, just like any other bride, and you'll be grateful all your life that you were married with a Mass." Were truer words ever said? And will I ever, in all my life, be grateful enough to Father O'Brien for his insistence regarding that beautiful, beautiful Mass?

Immediately after our wedding, Bill and I lived in a little apartment near his place of business, and I can't tell you the countless times I murmured, "Oh, God, if this is just a beautiful dream, please don't *ever* let me wake up!" It made me so happy when Bill said that he was happier than he had ever dreamed of being. "That's because our marriage is built on the firm foundation of love, respect and understanding," he'd say, "instead of the weak and shaky basis of infatuation or physical attraction that is wrecking so many marriages of our times." As one wonderful day followed another, I felt that it was impossible for me to know any greater joy, and then I found that God had even a greater blessing in store for us — we were going to have a baby!

Bill and I.

# CHAPTER TWO

## *Early Trials and Joys*

"You've got a beautiful baby girl, Mary." I listened to these words of Dr. McGeary's as I struggled back to the world of reality, and in this moment between waking and sleeping I remembered something Bill had said a long, long time ago, when he was the "boy next door" and I was just his crippled neighbor. "If I'm ever lucky enough to have a baby girl," he said, "I'd like to call her 'Billie.' Don't you think that's a cute name for a girl?" Oh, how I fought to be fully awake so that I could see my Bill and tell him that his little Billie was no longer a dream, but a reality. Of course, on our parish records (yes, she was baptized by our own Father O'Brien ) she is very formally Wilma Mary, named after her Dad and Mom both, but even though she's all grown up and married, with a baby of her own, she's still our little Billie!

Just like countless mothers and fathers before and since, we decided that now that we'd been entrusted with the care of our precious baby our apartment would no longer do. With much scrimping and sacrifice, we managed to raise the down payment on a small house in the suburbs and then our dream world was really complete. Each day, when Bill came home from work, Billie and I would be waiting for him. Who could describe the wondrous magic of those days as we watched our baby grow up? Her bright smile of recognition when we entered her room in the morning, her first efforts to toddle and finally her first precious words. By the time she was approaching her second birthday we were so happy to learn that she'd soon be sharing her nursery with a little brother or sister! If we had but known how God was going to test our love and faith in the months immediately preceding and following the birth of our second child, the joy that was ours at that moment would certainly have been dimmed.

Our family have always been very close, and the visits that my Mom and Dad and sisters and brothers made are among the happiest memories of those early years of our marriage. As the holidays approached (our first holidays in our own home) we decided to invite both of our families to spend New Year's Eve with us. I can still remember all the fun we had as we planned that party, and as our guests arrived and our party began, we had no inkling at all that this would be the last night of our marriage that we would be like a couple of kids playing house. Before twenty-fours hours had passed we would be face to face with cold, hard relentless death.

Dad and Mom, who had been daily Communicants as long as I could remember, had their last drink of fruit punch shortly before the bells rang in the New Year, and about an hour later decided to go home, since Dad had to work the next day. When I started to go to the door with them, Dad said, "No, dear, it's bitter cold out, and it would be an awful thing to catch cold when your new baby will be here in just a month. What would we ever do if anything happened to you?" And he kissed me and wished me all the joy of the New Year and he was gone. Less than twelve hours later, he was found dead at work. He had suffered a cerebral hemorrhage.

The days between Dad's death and his funeral were just painfilled nightmares. I attended his Solemn High Requiem Mass and the last conscious memory I have before I passed into oblivion was watching his coffin being lowered into its grave. I was brought from the cemetery to the hospital, and the weeks that followed are still vague and unreal in my memory. Early in February, when my strength seemed to be at its lowest ebb, I was given Extreme Unction and our son was born. The first real effort I made to struggle back to the land of the living was when Dr. McGeary told me that due to an unfortunate epidemic in the nursery our baby had impetigo and in fifty per cent of the cases such cases in infancy resulted in death. From the depths of my awful apathy, I began to beg God to spare the life of our tiny son. Bill was the one who suffered the most during those trying days. When I came home from the hospital, I wondered how he ever managed to hold up under all the responsibility. He took his vacation so that he could take care of our poor sick little baby, and when little Jimmy (we'd named him after my Dad) began to recover from the dread infection, the doctor told us that only Bill's untiring, ceaseless care had saved his life.

I wish I could tell you that the return of our little boy's health brought back the carefree happiness that had once been ours, but it was still early in a year full of trials and heartbreak. Early that spring, Bill became very ill and had to be rushed to the hospital for an appendectomy. After several weeks of convalescence, and just the night before he planned to return to work, Bill was coming down our stairs when the heel of his slipper came off, and he fell, fracturing the end of his spine. Since he drives a bus, this accident made it impossible for him to return to work for many, many months, and spelled financial as well as physical disaster for us.

While Bill was still recovering from his fall, I, too, had an accident. One day, while going down the basement stairs into our laundry, I lost my balance and fell on my face on the basement floor. My nose was broken and my face required several stitches. As this awful year dragged slowly on, and the late autumn nights brought the first frost, we knew real heartache again. Billie had often seen her Daddy wet down the coal in the bin to keep the coal dust washed away. One day as I was busy at the washing machine she opened the furnace door and threw a basin of water in on the roaring coals.

Her poor little face and hands were so terribly burned, and I found myself begging God in His infinite mercy not to let our beautiful little girl be scarred for life. And on New Year's Eve, just a year from our wonderful party, the final blow fell. We received a telegram from the bank holding our mortgage stating that since Bill's illness and loss of work made it impossible for us to meet our mortgage payments, and there was still no indication as to when he would be able to work again, they had foreclosed our mortgage and gave us thirty days to find other living quarters. As the bells rang out that bleak and frightful year, Bill and I held each other close, convinced that if our love and faith could survive so many and such frightening tests, then surely nothing could really lick us, and the future could only hold bright hope and promise of better things to come.

We still faced some monumental problems in that new year. First of all, it was wartime, and living quarters were hard to find. With two small children it was almost impossible, and finally we moved in with relatives. While they were wonderful and kind, it was an unhappy situation for both of us. Their children were grown and found it difficult to understand the antics and mischief that little boys and girls can get into. We finally found a house for rent, close to my mother, and to the relief of all concerned we decided to take it.

After almost a year of illness and suffering, Bill was back working full time and things were beginning to look up for us again  when the man from the rental agency came to inform us that he had a cash buyer for our house, but since we had the first option by right of tenancy  he would give us thirty days to make up our minds whether or not we wanted to buy it. With the ache of losing our lovely little home in the suburbs still fresh in our minds, and no conceivable way of raising the necessary funds for a down payment, we were in an awful quandary. The very thought of going through the house-hunting ordeal again filled us with dread, and so we began a real flurry of selling insurance policies and everything else we could get our hands on, in order to avoid the problem of moving. While we were not really happy about buying such a big, old house, it seemed the only solution to our dilemma and we breathed a prayer of gratitude when we were finally able to raise the down payment. If anyone had told us then, in all the worry and insecurity we felt after our first experience as home owners, that all these years later, we'd still be living in this big old house and that time would make it rich and dear with precious memories, I wouldn't have believed it.

About a year after we moved here, Barbara Anne was born, and less than two years later  little Mary arrived. Each of these events filled our hearts with joy, but Jimmy's comment on being told that he now had *three* sisters became one of the classics of our time. With all the dignity of a five-year-old, he said, "Gee whiz, Dad, don't you think there are too many women in this house? I'm glad my dog's a boy!"

Mom lived in the house next door with my sister Rose and my three younger brothers. (She and my brother Bud still live there.) Rose's husband, Frank, was overseas, fighting in the European campaign at this time, and had never even seen their little daughter, Joan, who was the same age as our Barbara. These two made quite a pair and managed to keep the two houses in an uproar most of the time with their mischievous antics. My two youngest brothers, Frank and Jack, were only a few years older than our own kiddies. Looking back on bustling, busy family days, it seems incredible to think that in just a few more months Jack will be ordained to the holy priesthood, and just two years later Frank, too, will be ordained. My older brothers, Jim and Joe, married and with families of their own, lived not too far away from us, so that all of us got together quite often. Except for the awful worry of the war and the constant concern over our brother Bud, and Rose's Frank, who were both engaged in active combat, these were probably some of the best years of our lives, although our houseful of kiddies kept us in some kind of a stew most of the time. I'll never forget the year that Jimmy started kindergarten. Sister had given him a tiny little cardboard image of the Infant Jesus, and he was thrilled to death with it. He never set it down all day, and insisted on taking it to bed with him that night. Later on, when we were going into bed, we made our usual last-minute check on the children, and the chaos that met our eyes in Jimmy's room was almost beyond belief. He had emptied his big dresser drawer-ful of clothes onto the floor and put the drawer in his bed. Then, with a paring knife he had slit all the stuffed toys the children owned and emptied the cotton into the drawer. And directly in the middle of all the cotton was the tiny, cardboard Infant. My cries of dismay awakened him, and he looked at me in shocked surprise, saying, "Gosh, Mommy, you *couldn't* be mad at me because I made a bed for Baby Jesus, could you?" What would you have said?

Then there was the time that Bill had just done Jimmy's room over. How well I remember all the hours he spent perched high on the step-ladder, doing that ceiling over and over again, until it finally satisfied him. You can imagine how he felt, then, the day he came home to find that Jim had glued holy pictures all over the ceiling. Jim gave what he considered a perfectly logical explanation: "But, Daddy, I love to lie in bed and look at them and think about God." And I can still hear Bill's protest as he gazed ruefully at the pictures, surrounded by countless dirty little fingerprints: "Well, couldn't you *at least* have washed your hands before you did it?"

I remember, too, the time Bill and I were going out, and my brother Bud offered to mind the children for us. Jimmy decided to take advantage of the opportunity to tease his sisters unmercifully, and when the situation really got out of hand Bud put Jimmy in the closet. He expected all kinds of roaring protests, and as the minutes went by without a sound coming from the closet Bud was scared that Jimmy was smothering. He opened the door and said. "Jimmy, if you'll be a good boy, you can come out now." And the answer he got still brings a smile to Bud's face. In solemn tones, Jimmy said, "Will you please close that door? I'm saying my rosary and you're distracting me." Funny, precious memories, but the tiny Infant and the holy pictures on the ceiling and the rosary in the dark closet that spoke of a little boy's love for Jesus all added up to this wonderful fact — in the very near future, Jimmy will be giving his life to his beloved Jesus as a religious brother.

There was another incident that happened around the same time that Bill and I often chuckle over, although it was far from being funny at the time it happened. Bill worked nights and I always waited up for him. During the week, I always got up early to get the children ready for school. Therefore, I looked forward with longing to each Saturday morning, when I could stay in bed a little longer. On Friday nights, when I put the kiddies to bed, I'd plead, "Now, if you *do* wake up early in the morning, won't you *please* play quietly in your rooms until I get up?" Sometimes things worked out fine, but there was one particular Saturday morning when they didn't.

For weeks and weeks Bill had been repainting the living room and halls. (Poor, dear, Bill — this big, old house keeps him chained to the paint cans and tool chest!) The open staircase going from one floor to another makes redecorating a monumental job, since the living room and staircases must all be done together, as they all open into each other. I shudder every time it is done, because this old-fashioned house with its very high ceilings really presents a problem. You'd know what I mean if you could see Bill precariously perched on a ladder that is tied to the staircase at one end and propped against the skylight at the other. With much reaching and straining he can just reach the wall that makes a sheer drop from the ceiling of the third floor to the bottom of the second floor.

On the week-end in question, he had just completed a second coat on all the walls — a lovely, delicate blue — and had bought the material to give the stairs and balustrades a coat of dark oak varnish. Since he planned to get into the job immediately after breakfast, he put all the paint cans, brushes, etc. in the top hall. The children's rooms were at either end of that hall, Jimmy's in the front and the girls' at the rear.

When I heard them stirring in the hall that Saturday morning I opened the door of our room on the floor below, and told them that it was still very early, and I wanted them to go back into their own rooms and play quietly. They assured me that they would, and I returned to bed to fall into that wonderful sound sleep that seems only to come when you should be getting up in the morning. I don't know just how much later it was that I awakened to a resounding crash and all sorts of commotion.

Bill jumped out of bed and headed for the stairs, and I followed him as fast as I was able to. How shall I describe the awful dismay that was ours as we saw our lovely blue walls splattered with ugly brown stains, and a veritable river of dark brown varnish flowing down the stairs to meet us. Bill started running up the stairs in his bare feet, and I was right behind him. My physical affliction makes it necessary for me to go up these stairs on my hands and knees, so you can just imagine the picture we made. It was like something out of a Mack Sennett comedy. Bill's feet kept slipping and sliding in the varnish and he was getting nowhere fast. Each time his feet slipped I would be splattered with a spray of varnish. In no time at all, I was covered with blotches of varnish. Even when we got to the top of the stairs, it took time for the realization of what had happened to sink in. The children, tired of playing in their rooms, had gotten together and decided to build a tent in the hall. They'd used Daddy's brand-new robe for a rug and their bed clothes for the rest of the tent. They'd balanced the broom and dust mop for tent poles, and what do you think they had used for ballast to keep the tent flaps in place? You're right — the cans of paint and varnish! It was clever and probably would have been lots of fun if someone hadn't gotten careless and stood up too fast, knocking the full gallon of dark oak varnish over the balustrade against the wall and down the stairs.

It was one of the rare occasions when they saw their Dad really lose his temper. He fumed and swung in all directions (even in all the confusion, I noticed that he made sure that he missed!) and as the children went running to their rooms, poor Billie slipped in a puddle of varnish and went sliding into her room on her back in a manner that would have done any big-league player right proud. "Don't any one of you dare to come out of those rooms until I tell you you may!" Bill shouted, and who could blame him, looking around at the wreckage of his weeks of work?

He took the can of turpentine and we both went down to the kitchen to clean the varnish off ourselves. What a sight we were! The varnish was oozing profusely through Bill's bare toes, and I looked like I was suffering from some strange disease, blotched as I was from head to toes. As I glanced in the mirror, the sense of humor that has carried us through so many tight spots took over, and I began to laugh. "Cheer up, Hon," I told Bill, "after all, there was no blood shed, and twenty years from now, this will be one of the funniest stories we'll have to tell of the children and the mischief they've gotten into."

"Yes," he answered ruefully, "and twenty years from now I'll still be trying to get this darned varnish from between my toes!"

# CHAPTER THREE

## *Enter Cancer*

While these years were rich and happy, there was a problem that I'd been struggling with alone that finally got too big for me to handle. In addition to our own four youngsters, we had a motherless little girl living with us who was just about Billie's age. The five children and the big house presented enough work to keep me going from morning until all hours at night, so that in the beginning I did not even worry too much when each day found my left leg a little more swollen and painful. When I was about nineteen, I'd undergone a "Corrective operation" at the suggestion of one of the bone specialists in our city, but unfortunately it hadn't been successful, and my left leg had been more afflicted ever since. Since I was on my feet more than ever these busy days, I was not unduly alarmed when my leg began to act up.

But when I eventually found myself living in a world of steady pain, I decided to check up on it. Without saying anything to my family, I went to our local hospital and had a series of tests and X-rays taken. I have only to close my eyes to see the sad, solemn face of Dr. Sprague when he finally told me the results of those tests. "It's cancer," he said, "Why didn't you come to us long ago? It began as a result of the faulty healing of your leg after the operation, and all the strain and walking on it all these years has done a great deal of damage. Your entire leg will have to be amputated."

After a few moments to let this dread news sink in, I asked him, "Will this amputation guarantee that there will be no recurrence of cancer?"

After a moment's hesitation, the ugly answer came: "No, we couldn't absolutely guarantee that. After all, you've neglected this problem for years."

I went home, sick and numb with shock. How could I tell this awful thing to my poor, dear Bill? After thinking it over for a while, I decided that I'd check with other doctors and other hospitals before I told my family. Eventually I was told that radium treatments might help, but that they would be extremely expensive. You can't imagine how heartsick I was, since our growing family and the rising cost of living ate up every penny of Bill's hard-earned salary. But I knew that no matter how much I wanted to spare him, or how much I longed to carry this cross alone, this problem had to be shared since it involved his life, too, and so, with a very heavy heart, I told him. How good and kind and gentle he was, as he assured me that he knew God would see us through, since the children and he needed me so much. How I wish I could have felt more assurance! The future looked bleak indeed.

And so began our second dark journey into debt, only this time it was my illness that caused it. First we raised the mortgage on the house to meet the medical expenses, then we took out a second mortgage. As the treatments went futilely on and the debts kept piling up, Bill took out one loan after another, until our obligations so far outweighed our income that I was sicker in mind and heart than I was in body. There were times that I even begged God to let me die before there was nothing at all left for Bill and the kiddies. But then Bill would hold me in his arms and tell me that nothing at all mattered as long as I was there to love and talk to, and as long as the children could come to me with their little hurts and problems — a job, he said, that only a mother could do. These were sad, trying days indeed, as I became less and less able to get about. Even my wheel chair was not much use after a while, and I began to spend most of my time in bed. Bill was doing a magnificent job of being both mother and father to the children and they were unbelievably good and helpful with each other. Dear, funny little Jimmy! I'll never forget the time he began to realize that something was seriously wrong. He'd come in from school, rush to my side and say, "What can I do for you, Mom? Want a drink of water? Can I straighten your bed?" One day he kept this up until I had to tell him, quite firmly, that there was nothing at all that I needed. "Gee whiz," he complained, "I told Sister how sick you were and she told me to come home each day and be good to you now, instead of crying about you when you're dead, and you won't even let me do anything for you!" And as if that wasn't enough, he came to me on Good Friday, put his arms around me, and said, "Mommy, can I please give you your Easter present now, cause I'm afraid you might not be here on Easter!" Wasn't he the little ray of sunshine?

Sometimes Billie's reaction was almost harder to bear. She never mentioned my being sick, but she worked like a little trooper. Although she was only twelve at this time, she had learned to master some fairly simple cooking, and since Bill was still working nights she'd come home from school and get supper for us with such efficiency that my heart would ache because she was growing old so much before her time. While Barbara and Mary were going happily along with no real change in their lives, and Jimmy was meeting the crisis in his own inimitable way, Billie was Daddy's biggest helper, and while I knew that she was doing all that she could to meet the problem, I had no idea that she was so aware of the complete seriousness of the situation until the day the door bell rang and a man named Vincent Seely asked to speak to me. He told me that our community had been conducting a "Mother of the Year" contest, and that essays by students in both grade and high schools, in public and parochial schools, had been submitted, and that because of Billie's entry I had been chosen as one of the finalists. Since I had no idea at all that Billie had even submitted an entry, you can imagine how complete my surprise was, and when I finished reading the copy of her essay which Mr. Seely had with him, I could not see through the tears. Such a beautiful tribute from my dear little girl made this one of the most precious moments in a lifetime full of blessings, and because no words of mine could do it justice, here is her essay, title and all, just as I read it that day :

## WHY MY MOM IS BEST

If you could only meet my Mom, I wouldn't have to say a word to let you know how wonderful she is. You'd know right away that she's the best Mom in the whole wide world.

You see, she can't walk at all, and yet we live the happiest, gayest lives you can imagine. There are a thousand reasons I could give you why she's different, and more wonderful than any one else, but I'll only tell you about the things that stand out most in my memories right now.

Once, when my brother, Jimmy, was smaller, he came home in tears, with his clothes all dirty and torn. He'd been fighting with a boy up the street, and when Mom asked him why, he said, "I had to fight him, Mommie — he called you a nasty name. He said you were a cripple."

I'll never forget how my mother smiled and took Jimmy in her arms and said, "But, honey, I *am* a cripple, and it isn't a nasty name. I used to be unhappy about it when I was little like you, and I couldn't do the things that the other kids did, but when my mother explained that God only asked great sacrifices of the ones He loved the most, I didn't mind any more. She told me that if I tried hard to be good and not complain or be unhappy about being crippled, God would reward me greatly. She was right, too, for He gave me a greater reward than I could have dreamed of. He gave me daddy and you children." She kissed Jimmy and wiped his tears and told him, "Remember now, the next time anyone tells you I'm crippled you be sure to say, "Isn't she lucky? God must love her very much!"

We were never punished the way other children were. If we were naughty, Mom was more concerned with making us understand why we were wrong than she was with punishment. I'll never forget the time my cousin and I had new coloring books, and we were having a sort of contest to see who could keep theirs the nicest. We were only a little over four, I guess, and Jimmy was not quite three. I was afraid that Anna Marie's book looked nicer than mine, so when she was busy playing, I gave Jimmy my crayons and told him he could color in Anna Marie's book.

When Anna Marie ran crying to my mother about the mess Jimmy made in her book, and Jimmy said I told him to do it, Mom shook her head sadly, and said, "I could spank you or send you to bed, but that wouldn't help you to understand how badly Anna Marie feels. Go and get your coloring book and crayons and bring them here." When I brought them to her, she said, "Now, give them to Jimmy, and tell him to scribble all over your pictures, just as he did Anna Marie's." I cried and pleaded with her, because I had worked so hard on the book, but she was firm about it, and I'll never forget how I felt as I watched Jimmy ruining one page after another. I didn't realize it then, but my mother had taught me a lesson I'd never forget about the golden rule, "Do unto others as you would have them do unto you."

Life is never dull in our house. Every holiday calls for some sort of celebration, and birthdays are always real events. But most of all, I love the Christmas holidays. I don't think anyone in the world has as much Christmas spirit as my mother. Up until two years ago, she could get around some on crutches, and each year, as far back as I can remember, we all went to see Santa Claus together, and it was almost as much fun as Christmas itself. We'd all eat in a restaurant, and we'd spend the whole day seeing all the lovely Christmas displays. When we got home, poor Mom wouldn't be able to walk for ages after, but she always insisted that she was the happiest kid in the bunch.

The first year that Mom couldn't walk at all, a cousin of ours offered to take us out to see Santa, and when we came home, Mom asked us how we enjoyed ourselves. "We had a terrible time, Mommy," said my little sister, Barbara, "it was no fun at all, without you."

That was all Mom needed to hear. On Dad's next day off, we set out, wheel chair and all, to spend our usual day among the holiday crowd. Nothing was going to spoil Christmas for her kiddies, least of all, not being able to walk. We went again this year, too. We certainly are glad Mom's chair can be folded up and put in the car, because even if Jimmy and I are old enough now to know who Santa really is, not one of us would think it was Christmas without our day out with Mom. Our little sisters, Barbara and Mary, still believe in the jolly old Saint, so you can just imagine how much fun we have.

Yes, holidays and happiness are very important to Mom. I remember hearing her tell my Aunt Rose why she feels like that. She said, "Raising a child is like building a house. The foundation is what really counts. Fill their childhood with love and security and happiness, then you'll never have to worry about the kind of men and women they'll be when they grow up."

I wish you could see my Dad and Mom together. They're like a couple of gay, carefree children. I know they have many worries, because of Mom's doctor bills and the cost of raising us children, but they keep all that to themselves, and let us only see the happy side of life. For instance, when Mom learned that she could never walk again, even on crutches, she and Dad could have gotten all upset about it. Instead of that, when she got her wheel chair, Dad had us all line up and salute our new "Wheel chair General," and Mom whizzed across the kitchen floor and said, "My, I never moved that fast in my life. The wind is actually roaring in my ears!" Then she showed us that she could move about as fast as any of us, and instead of that wheel chair seeming like a tragedy in our lives, it seemed like a wonderful thrill for Mom. Why, Dad even threatened to take her driver's license away from her when she ran over his toes.

It is always such fun to bring our friends home. From the oldest to the youngest one of us we know that Mom will make them welcome and glad they came. It always meant a lot to us, because so many of our little friends can't have their chums running in and out the house, but I never knew until just recently how much it means to Dad.

Mom and Dad have lots of friends, and they're always dropping in to see them. Mom is always ready for fun, and often I've gone to sleep with the sound of our parents laughing and singing the old time songs with their friends. After one of their get-togethers on a recent Saturday night, Dad met one of his friends coming out of church with him the following Sunday. I was with Dad, and I was surprised to hear his friend say, "We had a great time at your place last night. Gosh, you have no idea how the rest of us envy your wonderful home life. I'd get killed if I brought home a bunch of fellows any time I felt like it." Dad sounded so proud when he said, "Joe, I've been married over fourteen years, and every day of all that time I knew I could bring anyone home any time I wanted to. Even when I work nights, Mary is always there, waiting for me to come home. When I open that door and she's sitting there smiling, no matter how tough her day has been, I know that coming home to her is what makes everything else worthwhile." He sounded very sad, when he added, "I don't know how I'll live without her."

On the way home from church, I asked Dad why he had said that, and he answered, "You're a big girl now, Honey — almost thirteen — and I guess you'd understand a lot of things more if I confided in you. You must have noticed that each day it gets harder for Mon to get around, even in her wheelchair. Well, that's because she is suffering from a terrible kind of bone cancer, and only God knows how much longer we'll have her with us." I was so shocked I was almost sick, but I know that if Dad and Mom can be so brave about it, I have to be the same way, and Dad made me promise not to let Mom know he had told me anything about it.

But now, when I watch my wonderful mother laughing and fooling with Dad and us kids, just as though nothing is wrong, I beg God not to take her away from us when we love her and need her so much. Last night, she and Dad were talking, and they thought all of us were asleep. I heard Mom say, "After I'm gone, I hope they'll forget that the house wasn't always as shining as it might be, and only remember that I always had time to kiss their hurts, hear their prayers and tell them stories." Oh, if I could only put my arms around her and say, "Mom, dear, the house doesn't even count. What's really important is that you've kept even the tiniest corners of our minds clean and shining bright, our hearts full of happiness and our souls full of love for God."

Yes, as I said in the beginning, I wish you could meet my mother. You'd feel the same as everyone else who knows her — you'd love her!

*Wilma Mary Varick, Age 13, All Saints School.*

This precious, undeserved tribute from my first-born can still bring tears to my eyes, and when Mr. Seely told me that I was to be one of the guests of honor at a dinner in one of our large hotels, and that I would also receive some beautiful prizes because of Billie's essay, I could not help but feel that Bill and the children were the ones who should receive these tributes, because if there is something special and wonderful about our lives, it is because they have made it so.

# CHAPTER FOUR

## *Enter St. Anne*

The next few months of our lives were the most significant of all, and they are also the most difficult to talk about. I think they are best explained by repeating, in full, the article I wrote at the time for "The Annals of St. Anne de Beaupré," the official publication of the famous Canadian Shrine. It was entitled "Heaven on a Hillside," and here it is just as it appears in the Shrine records :

It seems hard to believe that there are many people in the world today who have never heard of St. Anne de Beaupré, and that there are many more, who have heard of it in a vague sort of way, as a well-known tourist site, or a place to which some of their friends have made pilgrimages.

To the thousands who have breathed the air of blessed Beaupré, knelt in the magnificent Basilica, participated in the beautiful candlelight processions, this little French-Canadian town becomes the symbol of all the worthwhile things in life. To those who have knelt at the feet of the good Saint

Anne, and through her intercession, have had God smile on them with blessings far surpassing any earthly understanding, this place is truly Heaven on earth, and they long only to spend the rest of their lifetime, telling the goodness of God and His blessed Grandmother.

It is to this last group, through the grace of God, that I am privileged to belong, and because I'd like everyone possible to know of St. Anne de Beaupré, I want to tell you my story.

During the first world war, when I was just eighteen months old, I was stricken with polio, in the dread epidemic that swept a good part of our country at that time. It left me paralyzed from the waist down, and while I was far too young to realize what had happened, you can imagine the heartbreak and grief suffered by my parents.

Many times I have heard my mother tell how she carried me, as soon as I was permitted outdoors, to St. Anne's church in Philadelphia, the city in which she was staying at that time. She knelt, with me in her arms, and had me say, over and over, "Oh, Good St. Anne, pray for me."

I am certain that baby prayer reached the heart of Good Saint Anne, but she knew, as we didn't that there would come a day when my need for her intercession would be far greater, and so I am sure that instead of granting the miracle that my mother hoped for, she granted her the grace to give me a full and happy life in spite of my handicap.

Only God knows how many times, during the years I was growing up, I heard my Dad express his desire to take me to the Shrine of St. Anne de Beaupré. But Dad's salary as a railroad worker was hard pressed to provide even the necessary things for his growing family of seven children, and although he and mother provided us with a home full of love and happiness, he was never able to make his dream a reality.

By the time I finished my high school course, (I was getting about on crutches then) I was just as anxious as all my classmates to get a job, and help make things easier at home, for these were times of great depression. Therefore, when one of the doctors at our local hospital told me he could perform an operation which would make it possible for me to walk without crutches, I jumped at the chance, although my parents begged me not to, since they had taken me to many doctors during my life, and no one else had recommended such an operation.

Seventeen long years have passed since I underwent that operation, yet I can remember as if it were yesterday the morning the doctor came in to tell me that it had been a failure. Not only would I be unable to walk as well as before, but my left ankle was set in such a way that my heel would never rest on the floor again, and I would have to wear specially made shoes for the rest of my life.

It would not be right to complain of the intervening years, for if I frequently suffered great physical pain, I also received the greatest possible blessing a girl could dream of. In spite of my great handicap, I married the kindest and dearest man in the world and our union was blessed with four beautiful, perfectly normal children.

When the pain grew increasingly severe, I attributed it to the fact that the kiddies and our home kept me my feet so much. Our lives were so filled with God's blessings that I was glad to be able to offer Him each day's suffering in thanksgiving for His goodness to me, and it never occurred to me that it might be advisable to see a doctor. But now, more than ever, I remembered how my Dad had always wanted to take me to the Shrine of St. Anne de Beaupré, and just as he and my mother talked, years ago, of the possibility of making the trip, now my Bill and I talked constantly, but in vain of our hopes of getting to Quebec.

Finally, my condition became so severe, that it was imperative that I consult a doctor. I learned, to my horror, that due to the unsuccessful operation, I had contracted cancer. If only I'd gone to a doctor when the pain first began to get severe, I might have had a chance for recovery, but because of the years in which I'd permitted the disease to advance unchecked, things looked black for me, indeed!

Why dwell on those years, except to say that each day found me a little less able to do the things I had done before, despite all that medical science could do to help me. Because our kiddies were still so young and even half a mother seemed better than none, I begged God not to let me die. Although I knew that we were financially unable to make the trip, and to do so would put us greatly in debt, I asked Bill to take me to St. Anne de Beaupré, because I knew if I didn't go at once, I would never be able to go. My wonderful Bill, who'd done everything possible to make my life happier than anyone's I know, was more than willing to make the trip, but by this time I was physically almost helpless and had to be carried around. Even the wheelchair to which I'd been confined for the last few years, wasn't much help any more. Therefore, if it hadn't been for my brother, Ed, who took the time off from his job, used his car, shared the expenses and the problem of carrying me in and out of the car at all the stops we had to make, we'd never have reached the Shrine of St. Anne de Beaupré. Mother, too, was responsible for our trip, because she took our kiddies, and helped us both financially and with her prayers.

The trip was a long and painful one. There were times when I was sure I'd never be able to make it. Finally, on July 17th, we reached the Shrine. There on a lovely hillside, sloping up from the banks of the St. Lawrence, stood St. Anne de Beaupré, in all its splendor. Although I'd longed to go there for years on end, I was completely unprepared for the majesty of the Basilica; the serenity of the town; the holiness of the very air that you breathed.

As they pushed my wheel chair up the ramp, leading into the church, I could not control the happy tears that streamed down my face. Although my Dad has been dead more than ten years, he suddenly seemed closer to me than ever in his lifetime, and through my tears, I whispered, "Oh, Dad, I'm *really* here at last!"

It would take someone far more eloquent than me to tell you of all the wonders of St. Anne de Beaupré. From the rows of crutches, hanging on the walls, each telling its own story, to the priceless treasures that meet your eyes on all sides, here is a place truly unearthly in its beauty.

Going up the hill, beside the church, are life-size stations of the Cross, and that evening as I listened to the fervent, heartfelt prayers of the crowd following the Way of the Cross, I knew that everyone who came here felt the presence of God as strongly as I did. Later, as I watched the crowd climb the hillside once more, in the beautiful candle-light procession, my heart was filled to overflowing with happiness and peace, such as I had never known before.

The next morning, before Mass, I went to Confession, and during Mass, looking up into the face of Good St. Anne, I pleaded with her to ask God to spare me to my family as long as I could be of any help to them. At Communion time, when God came to me in the Blessed Sacrament, I whispered to Him, "Oh, my Jesus, You know I have never minded being crippled, and that I willingly offered this affliction to You each day, in thanksgiving for the many blessings You have given me. But now I beg You to let me stay with my family and be of some help to them!"

All through that day I seemed to be living in a world apart, and even Bill and Ed commented on the unearthly contentment and joy that filled their hearts.

Now I come to that part of my story which I find almost impossible to tell. How can I, humble and unworthy of God's slightest notice, tell you of the moment during Benediction, when I heard Him call me, felt Him smile down on this broken, pain-wracked body? How can I tell you of that blank moment, when the universe stood still and I could neither feel nor think? And how can I tell you of the stunned moment of realization, when I knew that I was no longer in the wheel chair, but kneeling alone at the foot of the Miraculous Statue of Good St. Anne?

They *are* no words to really explain the beauty and wonder of that happened to me there at the Shrine, that night, but let me tell you that I have not been in my wheelchair since, nor have I ever enjoyed such vibrant good health. I am getting about easily on crutches, growing stronger every day. Do you wonder that I want to tell the whole world about glorious and good St. Anne, who is so close to God?

It is now several months since we returned from Quebec, and even yet, all I have to do is close my eyes, and I am once more in the blessed town of Beaupré. It seems to me that part of my heart and soul will stay there always, and we have vowed to return there next year, with our kiddies, and all of our friends and relations who can make the trip with us, in a pilgrimage of thanksgiving.

My whole world now centers around our plans for that trip. With the return of my health, I hope to be able to obtain some kind of work which will help make our pilgrimage financially possible, and as each day goes by, I know it is one day less I must wait until I can return to my own Heaven on a hillside.

That article was written over nine years ago, and in the intervening years, Bill and I have returned to the Shrine fifteen times, and brought hundreds and hundreds of people back to the feet of Good St. Anne. Our lives and the lives of our families have been completely changed by that first wonderful, unbelievable trip to her Shrine.

As for me, a very active life and a few health problems have caused me to return to partial use of the wheelchair, since I find that I can accomplish a great deal more that way, without tiring so easily. But in all these years, I've gone through several very thorough physical examinations, and there has never been the slightest trace of a return of cancer. So, you see, when I come at last to the end of my jour-

ney down life's long road, it is such a special grace
that I'll thank God for — health enough to have
enjoyed every minute of these growing-up years with
our children and handicap enough to have retained
my coveted place at the foot of the Cross, for it is
still my firm conviction that there is, in affliction,
a closeness to God never known or understood by
those who enjoy perfect health.

Ste. Anne de Baupre.

## CHAPTER FIVE

# For My Children's Sake

When we returned home from that first trip to "Heaven on a Hillside," we were just driving down our own street when the church bells began to ring. Since it was mid-July, we realized that the bells were ringing for our annual parish Novena to St. Anne, and so, of course, nothing would keep us away from that Novena. No, not even the fact that I had no shoes. A few years of being confined to a wheel chair or bed had found me no longer using shoes, and the soft felt bedroom slippers that I was wearing were all I had. Nevertheless, we drove up to the church door, and leaning on the arms of Bill and Ed I went padding up the church aisle. (At that time, I didn't even have crutches — since I hadn't been able to use them at all, I had given them to someone who needed them.) Father O'Brien was at the altar, and I can still see the stunned look on his face when he saw me walking down the aisle. Yes, it was the same Father O'Brien who had married us and baptized all of our children. For the past few years, he had been bringing the sacraments to me at home, and he had been completely aware of my failing health. You can imagine, then, how moved he was by the tremendous grace God had granted me  through the intercession of Good St. Anne. His letter, attesting to the facts in my case as he knew them, rests in the records of the Shrine of St. Anne de Beaupré, along with other documents verifying the fact that my recovery from cancer was, indeed, miraculous.

It was at this time that we learned that Father O'Brien also had a special reason for great love and special devotion to the grandmother of Jesus, it was because he, too, had been granted a very special favor through her intercession  many years ago. He told us that when he was very small, just about two years of age, he had, as small children often do, pulled the lace cover off a small end table, and in so doing  sent a glass picture frame crashing down on his head. The doctor who tended him  carefully examined and treated the wound in his head, and therefore it was difficult to understand why the following days brought increasingly severe headaches. Finally, his mother brought him to a nearby church and asked the priest to apply the relic of St. Anne to his head. After the application of the relic, the little boy put his hand up to his head, and when he took his hand down, there was blood on it. There, protruding from his head, in the place where the relic had been applied, was a long sliver of glass that had not shown up in any X-rays, and which would certainly have gotten to be a more and more serious problem as time went on, had it not been for the intercession of Good St. Anne.

The first days following our return home were almost like nightmares, for the news of my sudden and startling recovery from cancer spread like wildfire, and the house was filled with reporters, photographers, well wishers and curiosity seekers. We were so very grateful when the novelty wore off and we were permitted to really settle down again.

During the last two years of my illness, we had gone twenty-seven hundred dollars into debt. The house was so heavily mortgaged that we knew that unless something was done to increase our income we would go through the agony of losing a home for the second time in our lives. I told Bill that I'd like to get a job, but he protested bitterly. After days of arguing about it, I finally convinced him that since all the children were in school and he worked nights, thus being home for the better part of the day, if I could get a job for even a short time we could clear up some of our heartbreaking debt. And so, all dressed up in my new shoes and crutches, I set out to find employment, and even I, with all my optimism, was amazed at how soon I found a job in spite of my handicap.

How proud I was when I brought home that first paycheck, and I tried to ignore the rumblings of discontent that I heard among the children. Bill, too, was unhappy with the way things were going, but I consoled myself with the thought that he would soon adjust to the situation and when we were no longer so heavily burdened financially he'd be glad that I had been so adamant about keeping my job. But when, several weeks later, things had gone from bad to worse and my home, which had once been filled with laughter, was now the scene of constant arguments, I decided that the joy of our home was more important then any material gain, and so, over the protests of my employer, I quit my job. I had been corresponding with Father Philippe Lussier, Pilgrimage Director at the Shrine of St. Anne de Beaupre, who was with me on the night I got out of my wheelchair (he has since become Bishop of St. Paul, Alberta) and in one of my letters I told him of my unhappy experience in the business world. You can imagine my surprise when I found this editorial in one of the subsequent issues of the Annals of the Shrine :

## GREATER THAN WEALTH

Crippled for many months, and dying of an incurable disease, a pilgrim came here from the United States and was restored to adequate health. God spared her, through St. Anne's intercession, for the sake of her husband and several young children. She returned home radiant and full of great resolutions as to what she would do with God's gift.

But, she tells us, "During the years I was ill, our bills were very high. I felt it my duty to do something and succeeded in obtaining a job in a neighboring city. It gave me a sense of accomplishment, going to work every day, but evidently it was not God's will that I continue.

"Although our four children were in school all day, my husband did not want me to go out to work. First, he worried that it might be too much for me physically, and second, he felt that something might happen to the children, since they came home from school a few hours before I got home from work. But I felt that he would soon get used to the idea when he saw how much the extra money would help.

"And the children! Because they have always been so very, very good I'd always felt God had given them to me as a very special blessing to make up for my physical handicap. But from the very day I went to work they began to change.

"Since Mamma went to work, each of them felt that it was up to him or her to become the boss. Each night when I came home, instead of the happy home, filled with love and laughter that I had always known, I'd find four little demons, and a most unhappy husband. It changed me, too, because instead of being patient and understanding, I was annoyed that they seemed so ungrateful for all that I was trying to do. Wasn't I working just to make things easier for all of them?

"Then came a school holiday, when they had the day off, and I didn't. Coming home that night was like a bad dream. You can't imagine how I felt to see them all so unlike themselves. They'd been arguing with each other all day.

"That night I prayed to St. Anne for guidance. Suddenly, I could see myself back in the Basilica; I could hear my very own words as I prayed at the foot of the Miraculous Statue : "Oh, Good Saint Anne," I had prayed, "You are a mother, too, and you know how much my children need me. Ask God to help me, for my children's sake."

"How well that prayer was answered! Now, with equal suddenness, this prayer was answered, too. It almost seemed as though Saint Anne spoke to me; "God did not spare you to go out and earn money, but rather to take care of your children, who *do* need you!" Well, I quit my job the very next morning, and though our financial affairs are grave, indeed, our home is peaceful and happy, and full of laughter once more. I feel sure that since God has granted us so many spiritual favors, He will not fail us in our worldly needs."

There is a great lesson to be learned in the experience of this good mother. First things must come first. We are all prone to put material advantages ahead of spiritual and convenience before duty. Grant that others may see as clearly as she that no financial gain can offset the evil consequences of dereliction of duty.

A mother should be a mother first, other things afterward. If she tries to do more than one job, each will suffer. Each one of us should be content with the role that God has given us to play. Can we do less than give our lives as He wants us to?

You can be sure that this editorial brought me great comfort and upheld my conviction that quitting my job *was* the only recourse I had in order to be a good mother.

# CHAPTER SIX

## First Pilgrimages

And now we come to an entirely new phase of our lives. Do you remember my solemn promise to Saint Anne that I would return to her Shrine each year with my family and friends in gratitude for her goodness to me? Well, can you imagine the dilemma I found myself in that first year after my miraculous return to health? We were still so deeply in debt, we had no car and the prospect of getting the six of us to Canada and back (we had promised to bring the children, too, you know) was frightening, indeed. Up until now, we'd lived in a compact, happy little world, bounded on all sides by our families and a few friends. How would I ever reach out to people I had not yet met and convince them that, in all my inexperience. I was capable of organizing a pilgrimage that they would find both spiritually uplifting and physically satisfying enough to join us. But this was the promise I had made, and so depending upon the help of God, Good St. Anne and my beloved Bill, I set out to accomplish it.

During the day, when the children were in school, I spent hours writing to the railroads, hotels and to the Shrine itself for information regarding transportation and accommodations and the method of organizing a true pilgrimage in the spiritual sense. It was through these first letters that I got to know Father Eugene Lefebvre, who became the Pilgrimage Director at the Shrine of St. Anne de Beaupré when Father Lussier was elevated to Bishop of St. Paul, Alberta. Little did I know then that, during the years to come, we would become closest friends, indeed.

As the information I sought piled up, and I realized the cost and all the work involved, I was often frightened at the responsibility I was assuming, but I plowed doggedly ahead, without the slightest idea as to how I was going to cover our own family expenses. We had asked our relatives and friends to tell *their* friends, co-workers and relatives about our pilgrimage plans and see if any of them would be interested in joining us.

As the months went by, one by one, we would hear of a prospective pilgrim. In the spring of that year, since property values had risen a great deal, we filed a bank application for a renewal of our house mortgage, so that we would be able to make the pilgrimage ourselves. How many sleepless nights we spent while we were waiting for the approval of that application, and how joyous we were when we finally received the bank check, which assured our first family pilgrimage.

We planned to leave Grand Central Terminal in New York on a Monday evening and ride right through to St. Anne de Beaupré, so that we would arrive there about three o'clock Tuesday afternoon. We would then spend the same three days (and the same three dates) as Bill and Ed and I had spent there the year before. Then, by taking the same through-trip back, we would arrive home again on Saturday. When we took our final count, the day before leaving, I was thrilled to find that there would be thirty-seven of us in our pilgrimage group.

As I look at the picture of that first group, my heart is filled with warmth and gratitude when I see the dear, familiar faces of those who went with us then and have gone with us almost every year since. There's Anna and Johnny Fritzky, who have never missed a year; May Gnapp and little Andrew, who was only two years old at that time. Her husband, Andy, joined her in subsequent years, and they have missed only one year. And Vince Seely, whom I met when he brought Billie's Mother's Day essay to the house, and who has since become one of our best friends. He's been with us on several of our pilgrimages. Yes, there are others in that picture, too, who made several of the pilgrimages with us. How grateful I am to all of them for their trust in us!

"Ignorance is bliss!" Were ever truer words said? I wonder, now, as I look back through the years, had I been fully aware of the great resposibility we had undertaken and the complications we would run into, if we would have had the courage to go ahead anyway. First of all, you can't imagine the back-breaking scurry it was to transfer thirty-seven people and eighty pieces of luggage in the few minutes allowed for such changes from one train to another at Albany, Montreal and Quebec.

Then, too, while I had told everyone to be sure to have their identification papers for crossing the border into Canada, I had no idea that some people would take this information too lightly, and bring papers not acceptable for such identification. The most heartbreaking experience we've ever had in our pilgrimage work was on this trip, when one of our elderly pilgrims was taken off the train and held overnight in customs, because she was travelling on an obsolete alien registration card. You can't imagine the relief it was to have her join us at the Shrine a day later, after her registration status was cleared up. In addition to that, two of our pilgrims were travelling with only driver's licenses and social security cards as identification, and they were told that while they were going to be allowed to enter Canada with the group, they would not be permitted back in the United States without more legal identification. We sent telegrams to the City Hall in the city they came from, asking that their birth certificates be sent air mail, special delivery, to the hotel where we would be staying at St. Anne de Beaupré. I think that almost every moment from then on I found myself worrying about whether or not their papers would reach us in time for the return trip.

Our final problem came when we ran into the language barrier at the hotel. We spoke no French and the proprietor spoke very little English. After settling our group in their rooms, I went to him to tell him that we were expecting some very important legal papers for two of our group. He said, "I speak little English, so you must speak slowly." I wrote down the names of the two ladies who were expecting their birth certificates, and tried to explain that they could not get back into the United States without them. I told him that we might be in the Basilica when they arrived, as they were being sent special delivery, and that we wanted to be sure that he would accept them for us, so that they wouldn't be returned unclaimed. After several agonizing moments of speaking at a ridiculously slow pace, I asked him if he understood. He took the paper with the names I'd written, scratched his head and said; "You want a room for these people?" Finally, in desperation, we found a bi-lingual resident of the hotel who could explain our problem to him, but it was not until two days later, only a few hours before our departure, that the precious papers finally arrived.

Our ignorance of French was responsible for a couple of amusing incidents. Bill was standing near the Basilica when a man walked up to him and said, "Parlez-vous français?" Embarrassed and without thinking of what he said, Bill answered, "Me no speakee."

"Well, thank God," boomed the man as he slapped Bill on the back, "I've been looking all day for someone who understood English."

A few more such experiences convinced us that we would have to study French if we were to continue our pilgrimage work, yet here we are, all these years later, understanding just a few oft-repeated phrases. But the years have brought such warmth and understanding to our relations with our dear Canadian friends that we have learned to laugh off our mutual language mistakes.

On the whole, that first pilgrimage of thanksgiving was a wonderful spiritual success, and we returned home exhausted  but convinced that God would help us to keep our promise of returning each year. Since we had found the frequent train changes very trying, though, we made up our minds that the next year  we would try to organize a pilgrimage of cars.

We settled back into the routine of daily living, happy and grateful that we had been able to keep our promise to Good St. Anne. When summer was over, and the children had returned to school, I began to look about for some way in which I could help add to our income during the quiet hours of my day. A very kind lady I met taught me to make several different kinds of artificial flowers, and in no time at all  I had quite a nice little business in my own home. This source of income was to be quite a help with our pilgrimage expenses for the next few years.

In what seemed an incredibly short time, months had rolled by and it was time for us to plan our second organized pilgrimage. As I mentioned before, all the work of moving luggage and making train connections had discouraged us in planning another train pilgrimage, and we hoped to get a group together for a motor pilgrimage. Looking back, I wonder how I was ever so capable of such impractical optimism. While things were a little better for us in a material sense, we did not have a car or any hopes of getting one, and our family of six would need a whole car to itself. And yet I went ahead with this plan, confident that God and Good St. Anne would not fail us. I wrote to different companies for maps and other information, and since St. Anne de Beaupré was six hundred miles away, too long a distance for one day's travel, we decided to stay overnight in Montreal and visit St. Joseph's famous Oratory on Mount Royal.

During the winter months, May Gnapp, one of the pilgrimage group from the year before, whose husband was going to drive one of the cars in this year's group, heard the story of a beautiful Shrine, dedicated to our Lady, on the radio Ave Maria Hour. When we learned that this Shrine was located just half way between Montreal and St. Anne de Beaupré on the route we would be travelling, we decided that we would stop for a visit, and if conditions were favorable we would make an overnight visit there. We would then spend our three nights (once again at the same time of the year) at St.

Anne's Shrine, and would return through the New England states, staying overnight at whatever seemed the most convenient place.

My faith in God and Good St. Anne was more than justified, for just a few weeks before our scheduled leaving, a very dear friend of ours, Tom O'Reilly, offered us his car for the Canadian trip. After attending an early Mass on the day of our departure, twenty-two of us set out for our second pilgrimage. Driving to Montreal in one day proved to be a long and grueling journey, for it was almost four hundred miles away, but we arrived safely at St. Joseph's Oratory that evening. This Shrine in honor of the head of the Holy Family is a magnificent one, and we found every moment of this, our first visit to it, richly rewarding both spiritually and physically. We stayed overnight in a house right near the Shrine, recommended to us by the Pilgrimage Bureau. The next morning, after Mass, one of the priests showed our group through the Shrine, explaining much of its history and significance. To this day it has never ceased to amaze me that this great, impressive edifice is the result of the humble love of a simple Holy Cross Brother, who was just a doortender in a boy's school. How dear St. Joseph must love Brother Andre for his great devotion.

Later that afternoon, we continued our journey, and at about five o'clock we arrived at Our Lady of the Cape, the Shrine dedicated to the Blessed Mother that May had heard about on the radio. It was breathtaking in its beauty, and I'll never forget the warm and wonderful welcome we received from Father Renault, the Oblate of Mary Immaculate who greeted us on our arrival.

The ancient little Shrine is set in a park too lovely for description, and along the walks in the park are large beautiful bronze groups of figures, each one of them representing one of the fifteen mysteries of the Rosary. Sparkling like a jewel in the middle of the Shrine grounds is a lake, and on an island in the center of that lake, standing on a mound of beautiful flowers, is a lovely statue of Our Lady. During the summer evenings throughout the pilgrimage season, candlelight processions are held, and the highlight of these processions are the precious moments when the pilgrims stand around the lake with the candlelight reflecting in the water while one of the scenes in Our Lady's life is re-enacted on the island at her feet. One's heart and thoughts soar Heavenward during moments like these, and the cares and sordid concerns of the world seem far away.

A little brook runs through the Shrine grounds, and at one spot it is spanned by a bridge that would appear to be suspended from giant Rosaries. This bridge commemorates one of the most important facts in the Shrine's history. Many years ago, when the little Shrine was far too small to accommodate the people of the parish, and the cost of transporting stones for a new church from across the St. Lawrence by regular means of transportation was prohibitive for the poor little parish, the saintly pastor, Father Desilets, begged our Lady to permit the St. Lawrence to freeze over so that the parishioners themselves could transport the stones, with their own horses and sleds, from the quarry across the river. Although such a request seemed almost ridiculous, since the river currents were strong at this point and the river did not often freeze over, Father Desilets asked his parishioners to say the Rosary every day so that Our Lady would grant his request. Dutifully, they complied with the good priest's wishes, and all through the long winter months, a steady stream of Hail Marys by the faithful parishioners ascended Heavenward. But when spring began to approach and there was no sign that Our Lady heard their prayers, many of the people became discouraged and ceased to pray with hope. This was not so of Father Desilets and a few faithful followers who never gave up hope, and in mid-March there was a shifting of ice floes which left a bridge of ice across the St. Lawrence.

For eight days and nights, the men of the parish transported stones across this strange bridge, while the women of the parish said the Rosary. On the eighth day, as the last of the sleds safely reached the shore, and while the Angelus was ringing, the ice bridge disappeared into the St. Lawrence.

In gratitude for this miraculous favor, Father Desilets promised that even though the new church would be built, the little Shrine would never be destroyed, and he asked Our Lady for some sign that this promise was pleasing to her. There was a cripple named Pierre Lacroix who came to seek a cure, and together with him and a saintly Franciscan named Father Frederic, Father Desilets spent some time in prayer before the statue of Our Lady which surmounted the main altar, in the hope that she would cure the cripple as a sign that his plan was pleasing to her. The three who were kneeling there in prayer were suddenly startled when the statue opened its eyes, which remained animated for several minutes. While the cripple was not cured, he was privileged to witness, along with the two holy priests, one of the great manifestations of Our Lady's presence on this continent.

I wish I could tell you how I felt when I first entered the little Shrine and beheld this beautiful, miraculous statue on its golden altar, but it would take someone far more eloquent than I to do justice to that blessed moment. There is a truly great aura of holiness as she stands there in loving guardianship of her Divine Son, Who is a Prisoner of Love in the Blessed Sacrament in the golden Tabernacle at her feet.

There is one more thing I'd like to tell you about Our Lady of the Cape. Across Rosary Bridge, along the shores of the St. Lawrence, is the Way of the Cross, planned by the same Father Frederic who witnessed the prodigy of Our Lady's eyes. It is laid out exactly as Our Lord Himself made the journey so many centuries ago, except that because of limited space it is scaled to one third the size of the actual Way of the Cross in the Holy Land.

With so much to inspire one's heart and soul with love for Jesus and His Blessed Mother, I'm sure it does not surprise you to learn that we stayed overnight on our first visit, and have spent even more time at this heavenly spot on every pilgrimage since.

The following day we travelled on to my beloved "Heaven on a Hillside," where the welcoming voice of St. Anne, the Pilgrim bells, rang a heart-warming greeting to our little group. Father Lefebvre's sincere and wonderful greeting still remains one of the brightest spots in my memory of this, the second anniversary of St. Anne's great goodness to me.

The next three days were spent in prayer and great peace of soul at the shrine of the grandmother of Jesus, and it was with much regret that we finally left for home.

As we had planned, we headed down through the New England states, and as night began to fall we started to look for a motel with room enough to accommodate our group. After several unsuccessful attempts to find any one place with twenty-two vacancies (this was the height of the summer season, and we were travelling all through a vacation area) we began to be alarmed about finding accommodations. So, when we finally found a place that could take all of us, we grabbed it, without questioning the too-high price and the not-too-clean condition of the cabins. How many times we've laughingly told our friends of our experience at that place. "George Washington *must* have slept there," we've told them, "and they just couldn't bear to dust it after he left!"

We'd been travelling over hot, dusty roads for hours, and now that we had finally found a place, we decided to get together for a cool drink and a little relaxation before retiring. Since our cabin, which was the largest, as it had to accommodate our family of six, seemed most suitable for our get-together, we all gathered there. Later on, when we were putting the children to bed, we were moved to laughter again when we found that one of their cots was held up by empty pop bottles. We arrived home safely the next day, tired and happy, but much wiser than when we started out, and grateful that we'd be able to put our new knowledge to good use when it came time to plan our next pilgrimage. No more taking chance on finding last-minute accommodations. We'd make them in *advance* the next time!

Once more we settled back into routine, Bill on his job, the children in school and I back at my flowers. As I worked away at my potted geraniums, orchid corsages and mixed bouquets, my mind would be busy with trying to improve our pilgrimage plans. We were going to repeat our car pilgrimage, and Tom had told us that if his car was still in good shape we could count on using it again. Since we were reasonably assured of the financial means for the next pilgrimage, and our transportation problems seemed solved, I knew great peace of mind regarding our third visit to the Shrine. I was happy as the months went hurrying by, and early in the spring I began making definite reservations at the various hotels for our pilgrimage group. No more haphazard planning for me, I thought smugly, as I sent deposits in advance to assure our accommodations. I was quite proud of the experience I had gained in the last two years, and had no qualms at all in feeling sure that our third pilgrimage of thanksgiving would be the best of all.

"Man proposes and God disposes!" How well I was to learn the meaning of that phrase. Although I was not feeling as well as I might have, a few weeks before we were scheduled to leave for Canada there was no particular reason for any undue alarm, and so I went busily about packing and preparing my family for our annual "vacation with God." I still shudder when I remember my close brush with death, and I can remember all too clearly the evening only a week before our trip when I was caught up in a veritable nightmare of pain. Bill was at work, and my mother, who was with me at the time, called the ambulance. The nightmare continued as I was rushed by ambulance with siren screaming through the city streets to the hospital. I was given the last rites of the church and brought into the operating room around midnight. Several hours later, as I struggled back into the land of the living, I learned that I had suffered a ruptured tubal pregnancy, and even the doctors were amazed that I had survived.

A few days later, our pilgrimage group left without its organizer or her family. The money we had so carefully saved was gobbled up by doctor and hospital bills, and I was not able to leave the hospital until long after the group had returned from Canada. As I lay in my hospital bed, I was with them in spirit every step of the way, as they went from one place to another, to find the reservations I had so carefully made awaiting them. St. Anne knew that I had worked to keep my promise to her, and I was grateful that God had spared my life so that I could plan again for another year. But I had learned an important lesson. I would never take things for granted again.

Once more we were caught up in the school year and this was a special one for all our family. It was the year that my young brother Jack told us of his desire to become a priest and so he entered Seton Hall Divinity School. How fast the pages of time turn — he is already a deacon and in just a few short months he will become a priest of God, with His Holy help.

My own dear kiddies were growing up, too. Billie was in St. Michael's High School, Jimmy was in his last year in grammar school and Barbara and Mary were progressing beautifully in the classes just below him. The flower business was not as flourishing as the year before, but I had added greeting cards and nylons to my 'at-home' business, and I was grateful for being able to help in even a small way. Shortly after the Christmas holidays, we had the opportunity of picking up a fairly good second-hand Buick at a very reasonable price, so we felt well-off, indeed, as the months rolled around to the time when I began to plan our fourth pilgrimage.

Remembering our experience of the year before, each day found me imploring God and Good St. Anne to make the pilgrimage possible for us this time. Once more, I made all the reservations in advance, and it was with heartfelt gratitude that we started out with the group on the day scheduled for our leavetaking. It was the same faithful group of the last two years, and while I was so very grateful to them for their wonderful loyalty in joining our group again, I was just a little saddened by the fact that we hadn't added any new members — there were still twenty-two of us. The rest of the group had shiny new cars and marvelled at our courage (or nerve?) in setting out in our poor old Buick. I felt that Jesus, Mary, Joseph and Anne knew that this was the very best we could do, and that undertaking the pilgrimage in such humble fashion was, in itself, a perfect act of faith. Each day I begged them to watch over and protect us as we chugged along the dear, familiar pilgrimage trail, and when we finally reached the feet of dear St. Anne once more, I could not control the happy tears that streamed down my face, after the awful disappointment of the year before. Once more, each moment at her Shrine was filled with great joy, and once again, we headed homeward, spiritually enriched and physically refreshed after our wonderful "vacation with God." The old Buick did itself right proud, and brought us safely back to our home without giving us any trouble at all. When we pulled up in front of our own front door, I breathed a fervent prayer of relief and gratitude to God and Good St. Anne.

Back again to routine, but this time I was plagued with an unhappy feeling that, somehow, I was not working as hard as I might in keeping my promise to spend the rest of my life making Good St. Anne better known and loved. Here we were heading into the fifth year since her miraculous intercession for me, and in the last three years our pilgrimage group had not grown at all. All through the long winter months, this thought troubled me, and I prayed earnestly that, somehow, I would find a solution to it.

I had completely abandoned the artificial flowers, cards and nylons by this time, but I had found another kind of work to do at home. I was personalizing matches for the Ohio Match Company. It was a courtesy service they had for their customers. They provided me with a Kingsley stamping machine, tapes of assorted colors and several cases of very attractive, laminated book matches. When a customer had a new baby, they would send an order for a box of matches, blue or pink as the case might be, with the baby's name in gold; or when one of their customers had a wedding in the family, I'd receive orders for white matches with the name of the bride and groom and the wedding date stamped in gold on the match cover. I received twenty-five cents per box for this work, so you can see that it was not a very lucrative job, but each dollar helped and I was glad to be able to help at all.

Very often during the course of that year I'd look ahead to the summer with such a burning desire to enlarge our pilgrimage group, and since Bill drives a bus for Public Service I began to toy with the idea of chartering a bus. I knew that if I chartered a Public Service bus I could request Bill as the driver, and we talked it over, and decided that if we ever were able to undertake such a plan we would never touch the pay check he received for the job, but would use it to take either someone in religious life or some handicapped person as our guest. When we inquired into the cost of chartering a bus for such an extended trip, we learned it would cost almost a thousand dollars, or twenty-five dollars per seat in the bus. That meant that even though Bill would be driving the bus it would cost one hundred and twenty-five dollars for the four children and myself to make the trip by bus, in addition to the cost of our meals and lodging. It presented a staggering problem, but I could not stop thinking of it, and I soon found myself begging the Sacred Heart to help us with the plan. "You know how limited our material possessions are, my Jesus," I prayed, "and if You will find a way for us to get one hundred and twenty-five dollars over and above our regular income, which is already so hardpressed, I'll charter the bus and work so very hard to fill it."

It was then early spring, and I was beginning to plan reservations once more. Would I make them for the same group of twenty-two, or would my dream of a larger group come true? One day, as I sat pondering the problem, I heard a knock at the door. When I answered it, the man who stood there told me that he had attended a wedding the previous Saturday, and that each guest had received one of the beautiful white books of matches with the name of the bride and groom printed in gold on it. When he inquired, he learned that I had done the work, and he succeeded in getting my name and address from the Ohio Match salesman who had sent in the order for the wedding matches. He explained that he was so interested in them because he worked for Esso Standard Oil and they were planning a big convention, during which they were going to introduce their new Golden Esso Extra. He was very anxious to know whether or not they could get several thousand black laminated book matches with "Golden Esso Extra" stamped on them, for use during the convention. I explained that I just worked for Ohio Match, doing only the orders they sent me, but I gave him the phone number of the man for whom I worked, suggesting that he talk the matter over with him. A short time later, my boss called me to tell me that he had talked with the man, and because of tax problems, etc., Ohio Match couldn't get into outside orders, since the personalized matches were just a courtesy service for their customers.

However, he said that if I was interested in doing the work myself they would sell me the cases of black matches and the gold tape, and grant me permission to use their stamping machine. I would have to pay the regular wholesale price of the cases of matches, tax included, and I would have to come to an agreement on the price to be paid for the matches directly with Esso Standard Oil.

It seemed like a frighteningly big undertaking, since they wanted so many, many matches in so short a time. Then, too, with my very limited business experience, I had no idea at all what to ask for the finished matches by the case. After talking it over with Bill, we decided to trust in God and take the chance, and depend on Esso to pay us a fair price for the work. Ohio Match let me have the matches with the understanding that Esso would mail them the check for the matches and gold foil and give me a direct check for my work.

The following days I worked like a lunatic from morning until late at night. Since each book of matches had to be opened, individually stamped, then closed and packed, each night found me almost too tired to sleep. I grew to hate the sight of black laminated matchbooks, and I wondered why I had gotten into the whole thing, since I still had no idea of what Esso planned to pay for my work.

At long last, the wearisome job was done, and I was glad to call Esso and tell them to come and

pick up their matches. I told them the sum that
Ohio Match's check would have to be, and I told
them that I would be satisfied with any reasonable
sum for my own work. I hesitated to tell them that
I had no idea at all what such work was worth, and
therefore, I decided to depend completely on their
sense of fairness. It's impossible for me to tell you
how I felt when I looked, in shocked disbelief, at
the check made out in my name which their driver
handed me when he came to pick up the matches
— exactly one hundred and twenty-five dollars!

And so, in keeping with my promise to the
Sacred Heart, the next day I called Public Service
to make arrangements to charter a bus for our Canadian Pilgrimage in July, and I proceeded to make
reservations at the Shrine for forty people, the number of people the bus held. I hadn't any idea at all
where I would find all these new pilgrims, since this
was almost double the number who had gone with
us the last few years, but I knew I'd have to fill the
bus or suffer serious financial disaster, since we had
promised to run our pilgrimages strictly at cost.

During the weeks that followed I begged St.
Anne to help us find more pilgrims to bring to her,
and here and there, through friends, we picked up
a few new pilgrimage candidates. But all of a sudden we reached the Monday before we were to
leave for Canada  (we were leaving on a Saturday)
and there were still thirteen empty seats on our bus.
Frantically, I begged the Sacred Heart not to let
this first great undertaking of a bus pilgrimage fail.

"Oh, my Jesus," I whispered, "You know the financial heartache those empty seats will cause us, and You know that a full bus will mean that that many more people will get to know and love Your Holy Family better, for it is to the shrines of Your mother. grandmother and foster father that we will bring them. Oh, dear Sacred Heart, I am more than willing to bear any personal cross You wish to send me if only You'll fill that bus!"

I was surprised, the next day, to receive some telephone calls seeking pilgrimage information. It seems that someone who planned to go with us had told her friend, who worked on one of our local papers, of our pilgrimage plans, and the friend had written a small article about it, which appeared in that day's paper. How grateful I was for this unforeseen help, and I never could have imagined its result. By Friday evening, the bus was filled and we had turned away six people for whom we had no room.

On Saturday morning, our group attended Mass before beginning our pilgrimage, and when I held my Jesus, close to my heart in the Blessed Sacrament I could not thank Him enough for His wonderful goodness to us. A short time later, as I was boarding our bus, my foot slipped and I fell. I thought I had just twisted my foot and I was glad Bill had not seen me fall, since I felt he had enough to worry about with the responsibility of driving the bus, so I told people who helped me up that I was not hurt, and asked them not to mention the incident to Bill.

As the day wore on and we made steady progress toward Montreal, my heart was light and gay, but my foot throbbed with an ever-increasing pain, By the time we reached St. Joseph's Oratory, I couldn't even hobble about on my crutches, and I had to tell Bill what had happened. When I was taken to the First Aid Room at the Shrine, I learned that I had broken my toe. They treated it for me, and I spent the rest of the week getting about in a wheel-chair, but nothing could stop the happy song in my heart. How many people have the blessed proof that God had listened so carefully to their prayers as I had? Yes, even to the special cross I had offered to bear so that the pilgrimage would be a successful one. Many of those who were with us this time had never visited any of the Shrines before, and I wish I could tell you all the spiritual and physical joy they knew as they saw for the first time the magnificence of St. Joseph's Oratory, the unearthly beauty of Our Lady of the Cape and the holiness of St. Anne de Beaupré. With the money Bill earned for the trip, we had brought along two young seminarians who could not otherwise have made the trip, and several times during the week they told Bill and me how much closer they felt to our Divine Lord, and how much stronger they felt in their earnest desire to devote their whole lives to His service. This was more than ample reward for our small sacrifice, and the months of work and worry that had gone into the planning of the pilgrimage seemed as nothing compared to the happiness we knew in its realization. While driving the bus meant a great deal more work and responsibility for Bill, and the larger crowd meant the same for me, we felt, at last, that we were doing more to keep our promise to Good St. Anne, and we knew, even then, that we would assume the same responsibility next year.

And now the long winter months seemed to have developed into being just a dull, dragging period of time between pilgrimages and the days did not turn into weeks or the weeks into months nearly fast enough to please us. We made arrangements to charter a bus again, and early in the spring it was already fully reserved. It was with real joy that we learned that our very dear friend Father Bill Hornak would accompany us as pilgrimage chaplain this year, and we couldn't be grateful enough for this privilege, for it meant that we would have our own pilgrimage Masses and many other spiritual graces not enjoyed by those who are unaccompanied by a chaplain. How I loved Father Bill for being so good to us, and how eagerly I looked forward to this first pilgrimage of ours to be so richly blessed!

Two things happened during those months that brought our dear Canadian friends much closer. Father Lefebvre, Pilgrimage Director at the Shrine of St. Anne de Beaupre, came to visit us and it was like a visit from Good St. Anne herself, for Father brought along one of her precious relics. We loved every minute of his visit and couldn't thank him enough. He assured us that he, too, had enjoyed his stay with us, and that he'd be back again. I'm happy to tell you that we've had the privilege of entertaining Father here at our home several times since then.

Shortly afterward, Father Rinfret, Pilgrimage Director at Our Lady of the Cape, visited us, and while we had stayed at the Cape a few days on each of our last pilgrimages, this was the first time we had ever really had a personal talk with Father. Looking back, that seems strange, for since that time we have grown so close that he seems like a member of our family.

But this was the first time Father Rinfret ever knew the reason why the pilgrimages meant so much to us. We told him of our great struggle with our first pilgrimage by bus the year before, and many other details in the lives of the Varicks. Bill even showed him an article I'd written many years ago when Billie was just a baby. We'd laughed about that article many times, because I had entered it in a contest without telling Bill about it. Those were the early years of our marriage, and we were always doing a great deal of kidding about marriage being a fifty-fifty proposition. When a letter came bearing the return address of Bill's union magazine, he just presumed that it was for him, not noticing that it was *Mrs*. William A. Varick to whom the letter was addressed. (This was the magazine sponsoring the contest I mentioned.) When Bill opened it and discovered a check for first prize, he went to great lengths, reminding me that *I* was the one always making grandstand speeches about marriage being a fifty-fifty proposition, that he'd like *his* half of the check in cash, please. Imagine his surprise when I told him that I'd entered the contest and prayed to win because I wanted to spend *all* the check on movie equipment for his camera for Christmas, and that he had spoiled *his* own surprise by opening *my* mail.

When Bill showed Father Rinfret the old magazine with the article in it and told him the story behind it, we all had a great laugh over it, and Father asked if he might keep the magazine for a little while, since he wanted to show it to some friends. Of course, we agreed.

The Shrine of Our Lady of the Cape also publishes a monthly Annals, and it often runs feature articles on the pilgrimage organizers who bring groups to the Shrine. The March issue, dedicated to the sufferings of Our Lord, and stressing the thought that much good could be done if each of us would dedicate our own sufferings to God in loving reparation, was published shortly after Father Rinfret's visit to us, and he sent us a copy which contained the following article. (While it repeats some of the facts of our lives with which you are already familiar, I'm hoping you'll be patient with the repetition, since they are told in a slightly different way.) The article appeared as one of "Our Pilgrimage Promoters" features and was entitled "God's Greatest Gift" and began with the following introduction:

A living example of our theme, this month, that suffering can be put to good profit, will be found in Mary Varick. Her story, which is told in a general way in the article which follows, is one with enough meat in it to fill a good sized book. In fact, were we to consider all the facets of this action-packed existence, we would be hard put to jam them inside the covers of only one book. The philosophic maxim that "the idea impels to the act" finds its justification in Mary all by herself. She wanted to go to St. Anne's Shrine. She got there. She wanted to be cured. She was. She didn't want to lose her cross, for fear of losing its merit for the sake of others. She kept her cross. She thought it would be nice to bring others to the Shrines of St. Anne and Our Lady of the Cape. So she has brought them by the dozens ever since. She has had a great devotion to the Sacred Heart from way back. In fact, if she is Mrs. Bill Varick today and for the last 20 years, it was the Sacred Heart that convinced her that he was the right man and she was the right woman. They got married on the Feast of the Sacred Heart. Guests ate fish. So in 1956, to celebrate the Hundredth Anniversary of the institution of the Feast of the Sacred Heart, Mary decided she would bring a whole busload of pilgrims, charging them strictly the cost and no more, and that she would bring the six members of her family as well, as a Centennial Gift. With the money Bill earned for driving the bus on the trip, she brought seminarians, whose expenses she paid. When her bus didn't seem to be filling up, she promised the Sacred Heart she'd accept any cross if He'd help her. She broke a toe, business picked up, she had to turn people away at the last. You have heard of people liking to succeed the hardest way. Mary usually does take the hardest way, but she succeeds!

How does one tell the story of a love of a lifetime? Shall we begin at the very beginning? Mary Varick was one of seven children, born of devout Catholic parents. When she was eighteen months old, she was stricken with polio, and as a result, was left permanently paralyzed in both legs. In most cases, this would almost be the end of the story, but it was here that God's wonderful goodness begins. He had given Mary a mother with devotion and wisdom enough to teach her, from the very beginning, that an affliction was not an injustice or a punishment, but rather a wonderful gift of God's to those He loves so much. Is it not, after all, a very special privilege to journey through life, willingly carrying a cross that Christ Himself has bestowed?

That Mary was well adjusted to a life of affliction can probably best be illustrated by reprinting an article she wrote when she was twenty-two years old. It appeared as a prize-winning article in a Christmas contest sponsored by a magazine called the "Pilot." Here it is :

"There is no question about it — this is the time of the year when fairy tales have more appeal than any other. The beauty and mystery of the Christmas spirit fills the hearts and heads of the little people, and before anyone is aware of it, the grown-ups are right in the mood, too.

"As a matter of fact, this spirit has me so much in its spell that I'd like to tell you a story that I know. It's sort of a combination of the "Poor Little Match Girl" and "Cinderella," but it's just as true as true can be.

"You all know the story of the 'match girl' who made up her mind to be happy watching other people's happiness. Well, the little girl in my story is somewhat like that. You see, she's a girl who walks with crutches, and since no one could help her, she had made up her mind to always look for the nicest things in life, even though she was sort of left on the outside looking in.

"Now as the years went on, and this girl grew up, she dreamed of the lovely things that she'd like to have — a lovely home of her own, a fine baby, and most of all, her own Prince Charming. But, of course, things like that just didn't happen to girls who couldn't walk! !

"Ah, but that's where my girl was wrong, and that's where the Cinderella part of my story comes in. For one day, Prince Charming *did* come along, and he never even seemed to notice that his sweetheart couldn't dance. It's true, he wasn't dressed in shining white armor, and he didn't come after her on a dashing white horse. No, — he came in a little second-hand car, and he was dressed in just a busman's uniform. But, you can believe me, that he was more dear and kind and good than any storybook Prince.

"Today, they have a lovely little home in the suburbs and that girl wouldn't trade if for the most magnificent castle in fairyland. And their home is filled with the laughter of a tiny-golden-haired girl. The three of them are living in a world of happiness all their own.

"You say that it couldn't be true — that it sounds too much like a Christmas story? Oh, but it is true! You see, *I* wait each evening for this Prince Charming, in his busman's uniform, to come home from work, and waiting with me is our little golden haired daughter. Oh, I almost forgot to tell you, it's so trivial and unimportant amid so much happiness — I still walk with crutches!"

Well, Mary's happy world went on for many years, and to it, God added a wee crown prince, and two more golden-haired girls. While they never possessed much of this world's goods, theirs was the countless wealth of a happy home, filled with God's blessings.

"About eight years ago, a terrible blow befell them. It became increasingly difficult for Mary to get about, and each day found her wrestling harder with her ever-growing burden of pain. Finally, the doctor's verdict — she was suffering from a form of cancer which definitely meant her death in a few years at the most. The following months were nightmares of pain and doctors and hospitals, with no physical hope and back-breaking debt their only result.

In 1951, when Mary was almost completely bedridden, and had only a black future ahead, her brother asked her if she'd like to go to the Shrine of St. Anne de Beaupré. From the time of her affliction, when she was less than two years old, her Dad had always dreamed of taking her there, but the responsibility and expense of his large family had made it impossible; then death had claimed him before he could ever make this dream come true. Now, at last, there was a chance to visit the wonderful Shrine she'd heard about all her life.

Of course, the doctor strongly opposed the plan, warning that so strenuous a trip could only hasten her death. Mary's answer to his protest was, "You've told me that there is nothing more that medical science can do for me. What better way to die, then, than making a visit to God in this holy place?"

The trip was a long and tortuous one, but the spiritual peace that invaded her heart when she entered the beautiful Basilica was so great that she told her husband and brother who had brought her to the Shrine, "I want to thank you from the very bottom of my heart for bringing me here. Even if the trip should prove to be too great a strain, promise me that you'll never regret it, for this is truly as close to Heaven as one can get on earth!" Fervently she prayed to the Grandmother of Jesus to help her. "Oh, Good Saint Anne," she implored, "tell Him that I ask only to be allowed to live until the children are older and better able to take care of themselves, for surely, even half a mother is better than none!"

During Benediction, on the second night of her stay at the Shrine, Mary was in a wheelchair, close to the altar rail. She could not remove her eyes from the Blessed Sacrament, until she suddenly blacked out. Then came the shocking, awe-inspiring realization that she was kneeling at the foot of the Miraculous Statue!

Are there any words, in any language in the world to describe so thrilling a moment? And yet, even in this most important moment of her life, one thing troubled Mary. She sobbed to the priest who came to her side, "Oh, Father, I don't want God to take away the cross I've learned to carry for love of Him. All these years, He's let me hobble along the road to Calvary, in the shadow of the Cross, loving Him in my own special way. I don't want all that to change." And the priest told her that God alone knew what was best for her — "Not my will, but Thine!"

Well, has ever a prayer been so beautifully answered? Upon her return home, the doctors could find absolutely *no* trace of the dread disease that almost killed her, and she enjoyed a sense of physical well-being she had never known, but God had granted her wish. The physical handicap that she had lived with all her life was with her still.

Each year since then, she has returned with a pilgrimage group, in thanksgiving for God's wonderful goodness to her. During the year following her first pilgrimage, one of her group heard the story of Our Lady of the Cape on the radio, and ever since then, her pilgrimage group has visited the Cape, as well as St. Anne de Beaupré and St. Joseph's Oratory.

This year her pilgrimage group promises to be the largest yet. When friends ask her if she feels the effort and sacrifice, both physical and financial, are worthwhile, her answer is instantaneous. "Isn't it truly a wonderful thing for a family to spend their vacation with God each year? It's the most important thing in our lives! As for the hardship or difficulties involved, a pilgrimage trip always reminds me of one's journey through life. No hardship or tiredness or disappointment is too great to bear when one knows the spiritual joy which is the reward at the journey's end!"

If there is one message that Mary could pass along to others, it would be to all those who are afflicted. "How good God is to have given me this chance to love Him so. If I had been able to play like other children, dance like other girls, I would never have had the time to know and love Him so much. If He had not brought me to death's door a few years ago, I'd never have come to know the beauty and wonder of these blessed Canadian Shrines. Yes, from the very *bottom* of my heart, I know that this affliction was God's greatest gift to me!"

# CHAPTER SEVEN

## *Wonderful Privileges*

The day we began our first pilgrimage with a chaplain of our own was a very happy one for me. Father Bill said Mass for us in his church, served breakfast afterward and then we were on our way for our sixth annual pilgrimage of thanksgiving. The bus was filled to capacity and we also had a car with us, with six more pilgrims in it, so this was the largest group we'd ever had. During the long ride to Montreal, each time I looked across the bus aisle and realized that Father Bill was *really* with us, my heart sang a happy little song of thanksgiving. Truly, our pilgrimage was growing in grace as well as in number.

We arrived at St. Joseph's Oratory that evening, as usual, and the next morning we really began to appreciate the privilege of having a pilgrimage priest of our own. In previous years, while we had always attended Mass at the Oratory, we always felt just a little left out, as all sermons were always in French. You see, St. Joseph's is right in the heart of Montreal, and is really patronized primarily by the French-speaking people. When I wrote to Father Bernard to tell him that Father Bill would be with us, he had written to tell me that if we wanted to have our own Mass in the original chapel of Brother Andre we could. This is a very wonderful privilege we have enjoyed ever since, because we've been accompanied by pilgrimage priests on every trip since then.

I'll never forget that first Mass in the chapel, though. Our group filled it to capacity, and it seemed as though one could reach out and touch the Tabernacle, it was so tiny. Sitting here in this little church which was the first edifice which bespoke Brother Andre's great love for the foster father of Jesus, and thinking of the great, magnificent Basilica which dominates so much of Mount Royal brought home in an awesome way the power of love.

Seeing the dear, familiar figure of Father Bill re-enacting the drama of Calvary on this small altar, and watching his Mass being served by little Andrew Gnapp, who's been with us on our pilgrimages since he was only two year old, and realizing that our growing pilgrimage group was the result of our own poor effort to show our love and gratitude, made me feel very humble, indeed.

Each day of that whole pilgrimage brought special moments of happiness. Seeing Father Bill say Mass on the main altar at the Cape beneath the beautiful, miraculous Statue of Our Lady and again on the magnificent main altar in the Basilica at St. Anne de Beaupré brought us great joy, and as always these happy days passed much too fast, and it was with regret that we found ourselves on our way homeward much too soon.

But this was to be a truly red-letter year for us, because Father Bill's brother, Father Michael Hornak, who is pastor of Assumption Church in Jersey City, expressed a desire to take a pilgrimage group from his parish. Bill and I were thrilled to help him with his plans. Since Father Hornak could not make the pilgrimage in July at the time we usually went (due to his very special love for St. Anne, he was busy conducting a most beautiful Novena in her honor at the same time that we went to Canada each year) he decided to make his plans for mid-August.

Can you imagine what a thrill it was for Bill and me to be planning a second trip to our "Heaven on a Hillside" in one year? Yes, Bill was driving the bus, and I was organzing the pilgrimage for Father Michael Hornak. Some of our friends who could not make the July trip were joining us, too, so I was filled with happy anticipation. Bill and I were happy, too, because with the salary he received for driving this second bus we were able to take two more people who would not otherwise be able to make the trip. You see, we had promised God that we would always use any money Bill received for driving a pilgrimage bus for just such a purpose.

This, too, was a wonderful trip, full of special graces. It was the first time we ever had sisters with us, and Sister Marian and Sister Gertrude added much in both a spiritual way and in the general joy of the pilgrimage. It was wonderful, too, to see Father Michael Hornak saying Mass on the same beautiful altars where his brother had said them only one month before. Just think of all the happiness that was ours — two pilgrimage groups, each with a chaplain of its own, in one year. How humbly I thanked God for his goodness when we arrived safely home with our second group. Father Hornak had been very pleased with all the plans, and said that he would definitely like to plan to go again the following August.

And so, when we settled down into our usual winter routine, we had much to think about and plan for. We would be planning the two trips again, and during the winter months both Father Lefebvre and Father Rinfret would be visiting us here at home. Truly, our lives seemed to grow richer every day, and the harder we tried to thank God for all our blessings, the more blessings He heaped upon us.

Shortly before Christmas, Father Lefebvre visited us, and we were to see him twice again during the early spring. These three visits were happy events for us, and since I have a great deal of love for the blessed Trinity, three of anything always seems to have a special significance for me. For instance, on our very first trip to St. Anne de Beaupré, when just Bill, Ed and I had gone, it took us three days to get there because of my illness; we spent three days at the Shrine, and because of serious car trouble it took us three days to get home again. Since then, we always stay at least three days at the Shrine on every trip, and we are always sure to plan three Masses for our group during our stay at Our Lady of the Cape.

You can imagine what it meant to me, then, when shortly after the New Year, while talking to Father O'Brien (Yes, the same Father O'Brien who married us and baptized all our children! He is now the pastor of our church ) we found ourselves talking about the possibility of a pilgrimage leaving from All Saints, our own parish church, in the month of June. I thrilled to the thought of this Triduum of Pilgrimages, in June, in July and in August. I can't begin to tell you how happy I was as I was caught up in all the work of reservations, schedules, etc.

There was still another special, happy moment for me during those months. Father Rinfret came to visit us in March, and he told us that the Father Superior of Our Lady of the Cape had just come back from Rome, and he had brought me back the Papal Blessing in appreciation of my pilgrimage work. It was with the humblest gratitude that I received that precious document, and I prize it even more highly today, for it is signed by the late, beloved Pope Pius XII, who, I am sure, will be elevated to sainthood in our times.

With so much to think about and do, it was June before we knew it. Father O'Brien had hoped to go with us on this pilgrimage but a death in the family prevented him from doing so, and he sent

Father Denman, another of our parish priests, in his place. A week before we left, an article about our growing pilgrimage work, and the reason for it, had appeared in our archdiocesan newspaper, "The Advocate." As a result of that article, Mary Hafemeister, a very wonderful woman and mother of five small children, called and asked if she could join us on our June trip. She explained that she was suffering from lung cancer and that doctors held no hope for her at all, and that she, as I once had done, would like to implore God to spare her for her children's sake.

When I met Mary and her husband, Fritz, for the first time on the morning our pilgrimage was leaving, I was deeply impressed with their great love of God and each other, and I was almost as sorry as they that Fritz could not also make the trip. You see, they were not as fortunate as I had been, in having someone to care for their children. In order to make it possible for Mary to go, Fritz had taken his vacation so that he could care for their five youngsters while Mary was in Canada.

We were taking two of the best-loved sisters in our parish on this pilgrimage, Sister Rita Ursula and Sister Gabriel Maria. How I love them both, and how thrilled I was each day as I saw how much this pilgrimage meant to them. As our group set out that morning after Mass, I was sure that this must be the most pleasing group we had ever brought on our "vacation with God." In addition to Father Denman and the two sisters and Mary Hafemeister, there were two other handicapped pilgrims, so that at each of our pilgrimage Masses there were three wheelchairs near the altar rail at each of the Shrines. Yes, mine was the third one. Since there was so much walking and activity during each pilgrimage, I had to resort to the chair to be able to take part in everything. So there it was — my Holy Trinity again. On the first of that year's *three* pilgrimages, there were *three* wheelchairs, and do you want to know something really strange? On each of the other two pilgrimages, there were also three wheelchairs!

There was also something else very touching about this first June pilgrimage. I've been so busy telling you about our pilgrimage progress, I've neglected to tell you many of the happy events of our everyday life.

Our dear little Billie, all grown up now, had been married on the Feast of the Queenship of Mary to Don Adriance, a wonderful boy she had gone with since they had been in St. Michael's High School. It had begun as a happy high school romance, with Don a basketball star and Billie a cheerleader, and after each of them had settled down to adult life after graduation they continued going together. We were very happy when they came to us to tell us that they planned to get married.

Their wedding was a particularly beautiful one. They were married at the same altar where my mother and dad as well as Bill and I were married, and Father O'Brien married them, too. Jimmy served their Nuptial Mass, and Mary and Barbara were their bridal attendants. Don's only brother was his best man; therefore we knew the joy of seeing all of our children there at the altar together for this very special occasion. Since they were dedicating their wedding to the Blessed Mother on this, her newest feast day, Mary and Barbara were dressed in blue and white, and because their wedding day was within the Octave of Pentecost there were red and white flowers on the altar, in honor of the Holy Ghost. This pleased me so very much, since I had always encouraged a particular love for this wonderful and often neglected member of the Blessed Trinity as the children grew up. My brothers Jack and Frank, both in Immaculate Conception Seminary, had invited some of their fellow-seminarians to sing the Mass with them, and it was so very beautiful that just the memory of it thrills me, even today.

It was my brother Jack who teasingly accused us of thinking of the patriotic as well as the spiritual side of things. It just happened that the Feast of the Queenship of Mary was also Decoration Day, and the red and white flowers for the Holy Ghost and the blue and white dresses that the girls wore in honor of Our Lady made a very beautiful red, white and blue picture on one of our country's biggest holidays!

We were very happy when Billie and Don told us that they planned to go away on a week's honeymoon immediately after their wedding but that Don would save his other week's vacation for a month later so that they could go on our June Pilgrimage with us.

This brought both them and us a very rich reward, indeed. Father Rinfret, who knew they had chosen their wedding date in honor of Our Lady, was pleased to welcome them to Our Lady's Shrine so soon after their marriage, and on the day we were planning to leave the Cape to go on to the Shrine of St. Anne de Beaupre we were kneeling before the Miraculous Statue of Our Lady for our usual farewell Benediction when Father asked Billie and Don to come and kneel at the altar rail. He gave them each a prayer book containing a very special dedication of one's life to the Blessed Mother and had them read it aloud. He spoke to them briefly, gave them his own blessing and told them that he would pray that some day they would kneel in that same spot while a son of theirs would stand in his place and give them *his* blessing as a priest of God. It was one of the most touching moments in the lives of all of us. Olivette Richard, the lovely young soloist at the Shrine, then sang the very beautiful hymn, "Mother at Your Feet Is Kneeling." This was truly a precious addition to the treasure chest of memories that our pilgrimage years have given to Bill and me!

I had never been in Canada in June before, and I was so impressed with the loveliness of its springtime beauty, especially at Our Lady of the Cape, where one lives in a veritable fairyland of flowers and trees during one's stay there. All through the trip the weather was ideal, and Father Denman was such a wonderful chaplain. I had never really had the chance to know him very well at home, and I'll always be grateful for this time we spent with him, for since then we've been happy to be able to consider him among our very special friends.

On the morning we were to leave St. Anne de Beaupré for our return home, Mary Hafemeister came to me and handed me an exquisite solid-gold rosary. "I'd like you to give that to Father Lefebvre for me, Mary," she said. "St. Anne has granted me a very special favor and I'd like to leave that with her in thanksgiving." She explained that the rosary, which was very valuable in a material way and even more so in a spiritual sense, had come from Lourdes and had been blessed in a special audience by Pope Pius XII. I told her that since the gift was such a precious one I thought she herself ought to give it to Father Lefebvre, and she followed my suggestion.

Later, as we were riding home, Mary was sitting with me, and I told her how happy I was that she felt St. Anne had helped her so much. In view of her special gift to St. Anne, I presumed that she must be feeling much better physically. "Yes, it was wonderful, every minute of it," she told me, "and St. Anne is very good to me. She has granted me the grace of a very happy death."

"Oh, no," I protested, "surely Saint Anne has more than that for you."

She gently reached out and held my hand. "Yes, Mary, I'm going to die," she said, "but I am going to die a most beautiful death." I have only to close my eyes to see her face again, serene and peaceful, with a beauty all its own.

I thought of her so often in the days that followed, and we often talked to each other on the phone. She and Fritz came over to visit us one night, and he was so pleased because she was feeling so well. She had even gained weight and the doctor was so pleased with her progress. Since we would be leaving for Canada again in a very short time, it was natural that our conversation turn to the pilgrimage, and Mary told us she just couldn't stop thinking of the poor little children in the parish of St. Joachim near the Shrine of St. Anne de Beaupré. Since St. Joachim is the father of Our Blessed Lady and his church is in the town next to Beaupré, we always take our pilgrimage groups there for Benediction while we are at St. Anne de Beaupré. Since I've always been such an advocate of happy marriages, it always seemed a nice gesture to take our groups up to say "Hello" to the spouse of St. Anne, and I always felt that this special little recognition of her father pleases Our Lady, too. It is a very old church, priceless in its ancient architecture, for it is all hand-carved wood — not only the statues on the altar, but the very walls and ceilings of the church itself. It also has very old and valuable church vessels and vestments, some of them given to the church by European royalty hundreds of years ago.

But the town in which it is located is a poor little town, and the couples there have very large families and struggle very hard to provide the necessities of life for their many children. The kiddies, in their poor ragged clothes, had often wrenched our hearts, and through the years we had gotten into the habit of bringing pennies and goodies to them when we went to Benediction at St. Joachim's. Since we are the only group that makes this special little pilgrimage to their town, the children have grown to know us and our bus has only to cross the railroad tracks into their town and they start racing down to the church to greet us on our arrival. While we were always happy to bring them the pennies and goodies, it took Mary Hafemeister to think of their more practical needs. She said that she had gathered a lot of warm winter clothing that their youngsters no longer needed, and she and Fritz planned to bring them over the night before we would leave for Canada. With her own great problem, it was so sweet of her to be concerned with someone else's need, and even then I thought how very much God must love her.

On the Wednesday before we began our July pilgrimage (we were leaving, as always, on Saturday) the phone rang and a woman's voice asked whether or not it was too late to plan to join us. I told her, regretfully, that the bus was already oversubscribed, but she went on to explain that she would have been unable to go by bus anyway, but she wanted to know if she could go along in her own station-wagon. She had a little fellow, not quite two, who had congenital heart trouble, and could not travel without oxygen. He was very ill, and close to death, and since the doctor had assured her that whether she made the trip or not there was no hope for him, she and her husband had talked it over and decided they'd like to come over and meet us and talk over the possibility of making the trip. We arranged for them to come over to our house the following evening.

I'll never forget the first time I saw Clare and Art MacMahon. (Today, they are among our *very best* friends!) This handsome young couple seemed far too young to be the parents of four children — they looked more like a couple of youngsters out on a date. But after talking to them for a while and realizing the heartbreak that was theirs in the illness of little Darren, one knew that they were older and more stable than their years, and that God had sent this particular cross to shoulders both broad and brave enough to bear it.

When I learned that Art would not be able to drive up with Clare, but planned to fly up and meet her later in the week, and that Clare, who only had her driver's license about a month, planned to drive the long trip by herself, while Art's mother, who is a nurse, would go along to take care of Darren, I was stunned at her courage and faith. As it became evident that she had definitely made up her mind to go, I explained that the long drive right through to Montreal was a grueling drive even for so experienced a driver as Bill. (It's almost four hundred miles, you know.) Therefore, I suggested that she start out the next morning, which was Friday, and drive halfway, then go on again on Saturday after a good night's rest in a motel along the way. In this way, they would still reach St. Joseph's Oratory before us Saturday evening, and from then on we'd all stay together. This was the plan we all definitely agreed on when they left us that Thursday evening.

All that Friday, I kept thinking of this brave, young mother driving along the miles and miles en route to Montreal, and I found myself imploring Jesus, Mary, Joseph and Anne to watch over and protect them more than I could count. When Mary and Fritz Hafemeister came to the house that evening, with the clothes Mary had gathered for the poor youngsters at St. Joachim's, they too were very, very deeply moved by the story. Mary had been feeling well, and she and Fritz were attending Mass together every day. She assured me that both of them would remember the MacMahons each day, and would pray very hard that all would go well with little Darren.

The next morning, for the second time, we set out for Canada, and once again I felt that the group must be pleasing, in a special way, to Good St. Anne. Father Bill was our chaplain again, and this, in itself, made me very happy. We had our three wheel chair pilgrims, and now, in addition to the bus, there were two cars with us. With the MacMahons, we were fifty-six in number, the largest pilgrimage group we'd ever brought. And once again, the

Shrine of Our Lady of the Cape held something special for us. Andy and May Gnapp, our faithful pilgrims who had been coming with us every year, celebrated their twenty-fifth wedding anniversary during our stay at the Cape, and I arranged for a special Mass to be said for them. After Mass, they knelt at the altar rail at Our Lady's feet and repeated their nuptial vows. It was a touching moment for all of us, and brought special joy to Andy and May, since little Andrew, their son, had served their Mass. Afterward, we went over to the dining-room of the Pilgrim's House, where I had arranged a special breakfast for them, wedding cake and all, and to borrow an old but very useful phrase, "a good time was had by all."

My heart often ached for Clare and Barbara MacMahon during these days, for each day little Darren had attacks which necessitated the use of the oxygen tank they carried in the station wagon with them. It was truly touch and go every moment of the way, and I was often frightened at the thought of what might happen before we got home.

The ride from the Cape to St. Anne de Beaupré was particularly hard on the baby, for the day was hot and humid and he felt the weather so badly. I breathed a sigh of relief when he was finally tucked safely into his crib in the motel at Beaupre. How earnestly I prayed that he would spend a restful night so that his mother and grandmother might rest, for the strain of the arduous trip and the baby's poor health were beginning to tell on both of them.

It was about two-thirty or three A.M. the following morning when a frantic pounding on our cabin door awakened us. When Bill opened the door, Clare was there and asked Bill if he could find a way to get a doctor, since Darren was very low and not responding to oxygen. I went over to her cabin with Clare, and Bill went up to St. Anne's in search of a doctor. The baby's color was terrible, and I knew by the drawn expression on the face of Barbara, his grandmother, that she expected the worst. It was not until later that she told me she was so sure Darren was dying at that time that her real concern in getting a doctor was not because she thought he could help the baby, but only because a doctor's certificate would be necessary to bring his body back home.

In the meantime, Bill's search for a doctor was being hampered in more ways than one. Once again, he was plagued by the language barrier. He had a great deal of trouble explaining to the Sister on duty at the hospital what his problem was. She informed him that there was no doctor on duty, and because she spoke so little English she was unable to help him any further. He went to the Monastery in search of help, and even called the police to enlist their help in finding a doctor.

After what seemed to us in the cabin an endless wait, he finally returned with a doctor, priest *and* policeman. The doctor shook his head hopelessly as he checked the baby, and the priest stepped up to the crib and gave the poor little tyke his blessing. It was several moments later that we realized that his face was no longer blue, that he was breathing regularly and that the sleep into which he had slipped was a normal one. That was the last time Darren needed oxygen during the trip and for several months afterward.

A few hours later, during the Mass in the Basilica, I could not thank God and Good St. Anne enough for sparing Darren's life. It's a strange thing: only a week before, we were individuals, each with a separate reason for coming here, each with an intention of his own for which he planned to make this pilgrimage. And as each day went by, and we watched Clare and Barbara making their heroic pilgrimage for Darren, we became as one person, all praying for one thing — Darren's health, and all of us were richer spiritually because the MacMahons had provided us with the opportunity of praying so unselfishly for their little son.

When we finally reached home the following Sunday night, it was with a heart full of thanksgiving that we had brought Darren safely back. The following morning the phone rang quite early and when I answered and found the call was from Fritz Hafemeister, I was sure he was calling to find out how things had gone with the baby, since he and Mary had been so interested in him. So, I began to tell him, with great enthusiasm of the wonder of bringing him home all right, when Fritz interrupted me to say, "I'm sure that Mary must have helped you, for that is the day she died."

The shock was so great that it was several moments before I could speak, and even then it was so incredibly difficult to find words. Fritz said she was being buried the following morning and asked if Bill and I could come out to the funeral home as he wished to talk to us. Of course, I told him we would.

Later that day, as we sat beside Mary's coffin, Fritz told us of her death, and, as she had assured me only a few weeks before, it was truly a beautiful one. She had been feeling very well, taking care of the children herself, and getting to Mass and Communion every day. On Thursday, however, she told Fritz that she felt rather tired, and wondered if their parish priest would mind bringing her Holy Communion at home. Fritz called the rectory and the priest was glad to comply with her request. Although there was no noticeable change in her condition, she was given Extreme Unction at her own request. As the day wore on  and the weather was so hot and humid  (the same humidity that was troubling Darren almost six hundred miles away) Mary had difficulty breathing and the doctor suggested that Fritz take her to the hospital  so that she could receive oxygen, which would make her more comfortable He did so, and as the day wore on into night, she was comfortable, with none of the pain and choking or bleeding that is so common in lung cancer. Toward morning, she and Fritz recited many of their favorite prayers together, and early Friday she told him, "Jesus is here for me, now, darling," and quietly closed her eyes in death. It was almost the same time, up at St. Anne de Beaupré, that Darren dropped off into normal sleep. The doctor told Fritz that her quiet, gentle death was unheard of, since this type of death was usually an agonizing one, and Fritz and I both felt that Good St. Anne *had* granted Mary the special favor for which she had given her the lovely golden rosary. Bill and I went to her Requiem Mass the following morning, and as we knelt at the altar rail with Fritz, receiving the Blessed Sacrament for the happy repose of her soul, I was overwhelmed with the conviction that she was happy, indeed.

In just another few short weeks, we were on our way back to Canada with our third pilgrimage group, our three wheelchairs and Father Michael Hornak as our chaplain. This group had grown so large that we had to charter a second bus, and so there were eighty-four of us in all. Mary Hafemeister and Billie and Don's beautiful dedication of their lives to Our Lady had made the June pilgrimage special; and Darren and the twenty-fifth wedding anniversary of Andy and May Gnapp had done the same for the July pilgrimage. August was to be no exception. For the first time, my two seminarian brothers accompanied us and brought along two classmates. You can't imagine how my heart soared as I knelt in the dear, familiar Shrines and listened to those wonderful boys singing our pilgrimage Masses. This was truly a happy privilege.

And our outstanding pilgrim was lovely, lovely Yvonne. Crippled with polio at sixteen, on the very threshold of a modeling career and destined to remain so for the rest of her life, she was just twenty-one at this time. She had, with God's help, adjusted quite well to her affliction, but her parents, after begging God's help in the first weeks of her illness, became bitter when their prayers were not answered and had not been to the Sacraments in several years. Their only reason for coming along was because Yvonne had heard of our pilgrimage and wanted to join us so much, and they came along to take care of her.

It was early in the week when I first became aware of the bitterness that filled the heart of Yvonne's mother, and in an effort to explain my own love for the cross that I had carried throughout life I tried to tell her, as my mother had once told me, that it was only the ones God loved the most who were privileged to carry a cross for love of Him. "Did you ever think that her affliction proves that God loves her far more than you do?" I asked. "Since a modeling career for one so beautiful as Yvonne could quite easily involve her in so much worldly success and pleasure that she might forget God and completely suffer the loss of her soul, this cross she carries may easily be His way of assuring her Eternal happiness, instead of granting her a few fleeting years of worldly joy." But my arguments were to no avail — May remained unmoved.

"You may think this is a frightful thing to say," she told me, "but when God gives Yvonne back the use of her legs, I'll go back to Him."

Yvonne and I spent lots of time talking together, and I was happy to tell her how rich I felt all my life, in offering my affliction to my Jesus each day in loving reparation for all the wounds His Sacred Heart has suffered. "I like to think," I confided, "that as He struggled up Calvary's hill in agony, carrying His cross for the love of me, it brought Him some measure of comfort to look down through the centuries to see me struggling up that same hill, following His poor, bloody footsteps, willingly carrying *my* cross for love of Him." We felt very close during these long talks, and she told me that it would make her so very happy if her mother and dad *would* become resigned to her affliction and return to the Sacraments. I promised her that I would offer all my pilgrimage prayers for that intention.

The week, as always, moved swiftly along. We were at St. Anne de Beaupré, and our pilgrimage was nearing its end, when I told Yvonne how we always went up the Holy Stairs in a group. "I go, too," I told her, "but I don't think you should try, since it is really a physical strain, as you must ascend on your knees." She was determined to go with us, since she felt she was less seriously afflicted than I, and so I asked my brothers Frank and John to go with her so they could kneel on either side of her and she could lean on their arms for support as she ascended the stairs. I wish I were more eloquent so that I could describe the moving sight they made — this lovely young crippled girl, kneeling between the two young seminarians. I was not the only one who found this scene almost unbearably moving. Following Yvonne up the stairs on her knees was her mother, and as the tears that streamed down her face brought tears to my own eyes, I knew that the overwhelming power of prayer at the blessed Shrine of Beaupré was bringing some comfort to her aching heart. My own heart almost burst with joy when I heard, later in the day, that both she and her husband had gone to Confession, and planned to receive Holy Communion for the first time in many years at the 9 P.M. Mass.

Our group has always received so many wonderful privileges during our stay at the Shrines, and some of our group always received the honor of carrying banners in the candlelight procession at St. Anne de Beaupré. Because it was such a special spiritually rich day for her, I asked May if she'd like to carry a banner that evening in the procession, and she said she'd be happy to. After the procession, those carrying banners were invited to assist at Mass in the sanctuary, and they received Holy Communion kneeling on the top step of the altar. Can you think what it meant to me to see May kneeling there, and to see her husband at the Communion rail with the rest of us?

Later on, before retiring, May came to me and said, "I'm so very happy to be back in God's grace again," and then she added something I have never forgotten: "I can't stop thinking how much more generous He is than I am. I was so bitter and stayed

away so long, and the very first night I came back
to Him, He invited me inside the altar rail to receive
Him!"

Oh, blessed Triduum of pilgrimages now end-
ing — each one with its own special grace. How
can I thank my Jesus for so richly rewarding our
poor efforts to thank Him for all the joy we have
known in His Love?

At Our Lady of the Cape in 1960. Bill is standing behind me;
my children, brothers and nieces and nephews and other family
members are all around.

## CHAPTER EIGHT

# Planning for Afflicted

It doesn't seem possible that all this happened just a little more than a year ago. As summer waned, I thought, almost with relief, of settling down into our usual quiet winter routine, after all the excitement of the three pilgrimages. I could not know that I was just about to begin the most incredible twelve months of my entire life. I was to experience just about every emotion known to mortals — joy and sorrow; fear and elation; happiness and despair — oh, I could go on indefinitely. Looking back now, I thank God for one of His greatest and most considerate gifts to mankind — his inability to know just what the future holds. How wonderful that we can live only one day, yes, even one moment, at a time. I am sure that if I could have looked into the future and known just what the next year was to hold for us, it would have been so overwhelming and awesome that I would have felt completely incapable of bearing it. But how wonderful it is to look back on!

We had been seeing quite a lot of Fritz Hafe-meister during the summer months, since Mary's death, and when his position made it necessary for him to move his family to Tucson, Arizona, late in August, we felt a terrible sense of loss. He and his kiddies had become dear to us, indeed. Before leaving, he vowed that wherever he was, or whatever he was doing, with God's help he would join us on the June pilgrimage the following year, in Mary's memory and in thanksgiving for her beautiful death. Yes, we had already decided that with all the bless-ings our Triduum of Pilgrimages had showered upon them, they *must* be pleasing to Jesus, Mary, Joseph and Anne, and so, with their help, we would repeat them the following year.

A strange thing had happened in the spring before we had undertaken our first June pilgrimage. Father Rinfret was visiting us at the time, and we were sitting around the dining-room table chatting, when the phone rang. It was a crippled woman, calling from New York. She asked if I was the Mary Varick who brought pilgrimage groups to the Ca-nadian Shrines, and when I assured her that I was, she told me a sad story. For years and years she had been trying to visit the Shrines, but every time she had gone to a group organizer, he had refused to take her with him because of her affliction, ex-plaining that they could not assume the responsibility for a cripple, since they travelled so long and so fast that they were sure she could not keep up with them.

She had finally gone to the office of a group who conduct regular pilgrimages to the Shrines, and she was told that they, too, had to follow the plan of not accepting handicapped, but someone in the office gave her my name and told her that since I, myself, was a cripple, I would most likely be willing to take her along. I assured her that we'd be happy to have her with us, and when I hung up the phone I turned to Father Rinfret, in real indignation, and asked, "Father, how *could* those organizers turn away God's best friends? Are they not the very ones who most need the spiritual consolations these heavenly places give? It is at the Shrines that they receive the warm reassurance of God's special love for them. As a matter of fact, *most* Shrines have only become famous sources of spiritual comfort because of God's unearthly and miraculous restoration of health to these same cripples!" Father Rinfret, himself, was surprised to learn that it was almost impossible for an afflicted person to get to the Shrines unless he could make the trip privately or contact one of the few groups which accepted invalids. There was Andy Ahearn's well-known pilgrimage for the afflicted from Springfield, Mass., the Confraternity from Chicago and Louisville, Ky., Frank Suozzi's group in Buffalo, and Mrs. Sophia Nowosielski's group from Detroit. There may be some one else I haven't mentioned, but none of them left from our area. In the midst of all my indignation, I made a promise that was to change my whole life. "If God will give me the strength and ability to do so, I'm going to organize a pilgrimage that is planned primarily for the handicapped," I told Father Rinfret, "and I'm going to find a way to raise funds to bring along those who are unable to pay their way!" Oh, big and wonderful dream — Oh, dear, good, merciful God, Who made it come true. But, oh, those struggling months between the birth of that dream and its realization!

Just before Fritz left for Arizona, we spent a whole evening discussing all the ways of starting our pilgrimage fund for the afflicted. And as he bid us farewell, Fritz handed us a generous check to begin our fund. "I'd like to help others visit those wonderful Shrines," he said, "because of all the joy that Mary knew on her pilgrimage."

And I'd like to tell you about Anna and Johnny Fritzky, who have surely been our most faithful pilgrims. From the very first trip by train, they have been with us every single year since, and it was Anna who took over for me when the pilgrimage had to go on without me, when I was in the hospital a few years ago. We'd been affectionately calling Johnny "the co-pilot" on our July pilgrimage the last few years, for he brought along his own little bench, and sat right next to the driver's seat on the bus, helping Bill in any way that he could, and giving his own comfortable seat to another pilgrim. As soon as we told them of our plan to raise a pilgrimage fund, Johnny, too, made a very generous contribution to our fund. If only I could tell Johnny and Fritz how much courage their instantaneous vote of confidence in us had given us!

Early in September, we went to the Canton Tea
Garden, one of the best-known restaurants in our
city, to make reservations for a dinner-card party.
The only available date was November 4th, which
was a Tuesday and also Election Day. This caused
me some pretty uneasy qualms, since people rarely
like to go out during the week, and also many of
our friends would be busy on Election Night, helping
at the polls. But it was the best we could do, and
with a hasty act of faith  we signed the contract,
Bill and I. The next days were hectic ones, since
we wanted our fund-raising to be a registered, strictly legal act of charity, and we had to make several
trips to our city hall and to the state license bureau
of raffles and games of chance.

It still brings a warm glow to my heart to remember all the wonderful cooperation and help we
received from everyone we contacted in those early
days of our work. I'd especially like to offer a vote
of thanks to Joe Tyrrell in the City Hall for all he
has done and is still doing for our group.

Bill and I had found, during our recent pilgrimages, how very much the handicapped enjoyed getting to Mass, and had often talked of the possibility
of not only taking them on an annual pilgrimage
to the Canadian Shrines, but of taking them to Mass,
Confession and Communion at least once a month.
We could plan some sort of breakfast or luncheon
after Mass, so that we'd be providing them with a
little social joy as well as spiritual happiness. Remembering our Lady's Fatima requests  regarding

the first Saturdays of each month, and resolving definitely to make those consecutive First Saturdays
with our invalid group, we became the First Saturday Club, dedicating all our efforts for God's beloved
afflicted to Our Lady in reparation, as she had implored the children of Fatima to do.

Our many friends and pilgrims offered to help
us in our work, and our great dream was under way.
As soon as we were a licensed group, we decided
to raffle off a fully paid pilgrimage for two. How
appropriate, I thought, to raise funds to bring the
invalids to the Shrines by raffling off a pilgrimage
for some well folks to go, too. It just happened that
Father Rinfret was visiting us when we picked up
the raffle books for the pilgrimage from the printers.
He said, "I want to take a book, and if I should
win, you can have that trip for two for your invalids." He handed me a Canadian dollar, and I
told him, "Father, if all goes well, and God gives
us the grace to bring our invalids to Our Lady's
Shrine, I am going to use this dollar to light a candle
of thanksgiving at Our Lady's feet." From then on,
whenever our goal seemed unattainable, I'd look at
that Canadian dollar and remember my promise, and
somehow things wouldn't seem so difficult.

If you've ever run a card party, then you know
all the work involved in collecting prizes, selling
tickets, etc. Gosh, I can't even begin to tell all the
wonderful help we received. After all my worrying
about the night of our card party being an unfavor-
able one, I was shocked to find that the place was

completely sold out, and that the management of the Canton Tea Garden had to turn scores of people away. I had never seen so many beautiful prizes, all donated by well-wishers, and the table prize we had chosen had its own special significance for us. It was the statue of Our Lady of Fatima, which contained the family rosary in its base. I've always been happy that we were responsible for distributing over three hundred of those family rosaries, and I often pray that they are being used by the families that have them.

When the affair was over and we sat down, tired and happy, to check the results, we were thrilled, indeed, to learn that we now had almost two thousand dollars in our pilgrimage fund. I had done a great deal of checking, and knew that we needed approximately five thousand dollars to cover the cost of Pullman transportation, meals and lodging for the invalids we planned to take. But I had never even hoped to have so much of it raised so soon. A good part of the money on hand had been realized through the raffling off of the pilgrimage for two. The winner had been chosen during the evening of the card party, and this too had brought me a great deal of happiness. You see, because all our pilgrimage work was based on a deep and sincere love for God, I worried a little when we decided to raffle off the pilgrimage trip, for fear that the winner might be someone who would not feel the same way as we did. How earnestly I begged God to be sure that the winner would appreciate the pilgrimage most of all for its spiritual beauty. My prayers were beautifully answered when the winner was so grateful for the trip that she told me that she was going to invite a very dear friend of hers, a missionary priest, to be her guest on the pilgrimage. How grateful I was to hear this, for I knew that such pilgrims would be a wonderful addition to our group.

We were still basking in the happiness of our great success when one of those blows fell that only God understands. One morning, our phone rang and it was Don to tell us that their apartment had been ransacked. They were waiting for the police, and Don asked if Bill and I would come up, because he was so worried about the awful shock it had been to Billie, who was expecting their first baby.

I was heartsick when we arrived at their apartment and realized how great their loss was. Because her hands were swollen with pregnancy, Billie had taken off both her diamond wedding band and solitaire. Both were gone, and so was her watch and Don's cuff links and tie clasp. Her luggage, portable typewriter, silver service for twelve, electric appliances and Don's camera had all been taken, and more than two hundred dollars in cash, which they had planned to put in the bank the next day. In all, their loss totalled well over two thousand dollars, a blow which would have staggered any one, and these two youngsters had been married less than a year.

Because of Billie's condition, and the shock the whole thing had been to her, we were glad that she and Don decided to come and stay with us for a while. The police told them that it was definitely the work of a professional thief, and they, too, thought it wiser for them to come home with us for a while, since Don worked nights and it was inadvisable to leave Billie alone.

A little later that same day, Billie and Don went out for a while, and when they returned and I asked where they had been, Billie's answer startled me, and I felt a warm glow of pride in these wonderful youngsters of ours. "We went over to church to light a candle and say a prayer for the thief, Mom," she told me, "He *really* needs help, and if someone doesn't pray for him, he'll surely go to Hell." How many of us could have been so truly charitable in the face of so great a loss?

Billie was never able to return to that apartment, though. She and Don stayed with us until they found another place to live, and we were all happier when they moved into very nice rooms in a two-family house, instead of the cold impersonal rooms in an apartment house.

Before we knew it the Christmas holidays were upon us, and one of the nicest things about these holidays was that Yvonne, our very special August pilgrim, spent a good part of them with us. She had visited frequently since the pilgrimage, and we grew fonder of her all the time. I guess one of the nicest things about our pilgrimage family is that even though it had grown so rapidly, most of us managed to keep in close touch.

With the coming of the New Year, I was caught up once more in plans and work for our three Canadian trips. Yes, we had planned the bus pilgrimages for June and July, and we were having our very special one for the invalids in August. This plan was made so that we could leave on Our Lady's feast day (August 15) and by making it our usual nine-day pilgrimage  we would be at the Shrine of St. Anne de Beaupré for Shut-ins' Day, a very special annual event  when they had the Solemn Blessing of the Sick, at which each invalid present in the Shrine was individually blessed with the Blessed Sacrament. Since we planned to take some very seriously afflicted people  who couldn't possibly make the long trip by bus, we were planning this pilgrimage by Pullman. Thus, we could tuck them into their sleeping quarters Saturday evening in Grand Central Terminal, and they would wake up the next morning in Canada. You can imagine that plans like these really required advance work, and so these were busy days for me.

The New Year was not too many weeks old when we received a call from Art MacMahon. It was strange — I knew before he told me — little Darren had gone Home, and even in those first moments I thought of Mary Hafemeister. I was sure she'd be close by to welcome him. There was so little I could say to Art at the time, but a little later that day I wrote a note to Clare and him, telling them how grateful we all were for the terrific sacrifice they had made in joining us on the pilgrimage the summer before, because in so doing they had given us all a saint for a friend. Darren's brief sinless life, so full of suffering, surely merited him a special place in Heaven, and it was truly a privilege to have shared that life in even a little way. I told Clare that while I knew her heartache was great at the moment, hers was a blessing that I would have been grateful for — to be the mother of a beautiful soul that went back to God without ever having offended Him by even the littlest venial sin.

We went to Darren's very beautiful Mass of the Angels and as we went to Holy Communion I thanked my Jesus for this new, special friend in Heaven, for I knew we could pray *to* Darren, not for him.

As spring drew near, we had to plan another fund-raising affair for our pilgrimage fund, and we decided to have a spring dance. As we went about the business of reserving a hall, and hiring an orchestra, and taking care of the other necessary details that go with such an affair, my silly sense of humor often found me chuckling at a gal who could never really *walk* planning a *dance* so a lot of invalids could *ride* to Canada. When we were able to reserve the Community Center for the Saturday night after Easter I was positively gleeful, because I was so sure that after forty days of penance every one would be happy to step out on that first Saturday after Lent; therefore we could be absolutely sure of a great success.

I've never been able to figure out the whole thing. When I was so sure that our card party, because it was on a week night (and election night at that), wouldn't draw a crowd, it was a sellout. When I was equally sure that our spring dance would be mobbed because I thought the first Saturday after Lent was a perfect night for such an affair, every other organization in existence, including the Knights of Columbus, the P.B.A., the Democratic Club, the Republican Club and lots of clubs I never even heard of, all picked that same Saturday as being an ideal night for *their* affairs. Our poor, new little First Saturday Club found the competition far too heavy, and while our dance was not a failure (as a matter of fact, it was a terrific *social* success, since it gave all our pilgrim family a chance to spend an evening together) it was far from being the financial success that our card party was. Just goes to show you — one never knows, does one?

Once again, a good part of the money taken in was a result of the second raffle of a fully paid pilgrimage for two, and once again I'd prayed fervently that it would be won by someone who would appreciate it. And once again that prayer was answered, for the woman who won had been born in Canada, and had been praying that God would make it possible for her to go back for a visit. The trip was for two, and since she was going to make the trip by herself, she gave us back the cost of the second pilgrim, for one of our afflicted. How grateful we were — I'm sure God will reward her generosity in some special way!

We had been talking about our First Saturday Masses for some time now, and while most of our group had been attending the sacraments privately on the First Saturday of each month, we had not yet done so as a group. When I learned that Father Rinfret expected to be in the United States around the early part of March and planned to visit, I wrote and asked him if he would say a special Mass for us on the First Saturday of the month. "What could be more wonderful or fitting," I wrote, "than our Lady's Good Will Ambassador saying Mass for Our Lady's First Saturday Club?" Father Rinfret replied that he'd be glad to say the Mass for us, and Father Bill Hornak, who is the spiritual advisor of our group, offered his church for the Mass and his auditorium for the breakfast which was to follow. As we made plans for this very special event, I was so very happy because at last we were going to begin one of the most important functions of our dream.

Everything went along beautifully until approximately nine P.M. the night before our Mass. The phone rang, and when I answered and a strange voice asked to speak to me, I can't even begin to explain how I felt when the voice said, "This is Father Kennette, of St. Jean Baptiste Church in New York. I'm calling for Father Rinfret. He is here in the rectory, and has contracted a virus infection. He is running a very high temperature and will be unable to say your Mass in the morning."

"Oh, no! Not Father Rinfret! He hasn't failed to keep an appointment that he's made in all the years since I've known him! And where can I possibly find a priest to say that Mass at this hour? Every priest I know will already be committed to say a previously scheduled Mass. We've got over a hundred people coming to Mass and breakfast in the morning, and I can't even reach all of them at this hour, even if I wanted to postpone it — and I *don't* want to!" When Father Kennette finally succeeded in interrupting my tirade long enough to tell me that Father Rinfret had suggested that I call his good friend, Father Livolsi in Union City, to ask him to fill in as celebrant and speaker for us (yes, Father Rinfret had also been scheduled to be our Communion Breakfast speaker) he told me that if I couldn't reach Father Livolsi, I was to call him back. He gave me the number, and with a sinking heart and the firm conviction that the whole bottom had fallen out of the world, I hung up. Oh, me, of little faith!

I reached Father Livolsi all right, and he said he'd be happy to speak at our breakfast, but he couldn't say the Mass as he had already been assigned to a scheduled Mass in his parish. I called the rectory of St. Jean Baptiste and when the voice of Father Kennette answered (how I've grown to love that great, booming voice since then, and the infectious laugh that goes with it!) I told him, with all sorts of weeping and gnashing of teeth, that Father Livolsi could not say our Mass. (And how I silently cursed the bug that had bitten Father Rinfret!) Father Kennette told me that while I had been talking on the phone at this end, he'd asked Father Superior's permission to say the Mass for us and Father Superior had agreed as long as Father Kennette found someone to say the Mass for which he'd been scheduled. Well, after some more plain and fancy burning up of the telephone wires, everything was finally settled — Father Kennette would say the Mass for us.

It was with all sorts of misgivings that I set out for Father Bill's church the next morning. Our first real effort to fulfill our First Saturday Club promise — what a mess! I had never met either Father Livolsi *or* Father Kennette! How could I know either one of them? And how could such a haphazard affair be a success? How often I've apologized to Jesus, Mary, Joseph and Anne since then for my poor weak faith. The Mass was beautiful and so well attended — and everyone loved Father Kennette at first sight! And Father Livolsi, a truly gifted speaker, moved the hearts of everyone of us with his very beautiful talk on devotion to the Blessed Mother. Father Bill's wonderful parishioners were so gracious in serving us breakfast and Father Bill himself was, as always, so good and kind to all of us that in all our first breakfast could not have been more of a success under any circumstances whatsoever. There was an added thrill for me, too. In addition to my Bill and Jimmy and Mary and Barbara kneeling at the altar rail with me at Communion time, there was my dear, dear Billie, holding her tiny son in her arms. Yes, I am a grandmother now. Is there no end to God's wonderful goodness to me?

A few days later, we received a call from Father Rinfret. Fully recovered from his bout with virus, he was on his way to visit some friends in Connecticutt, Mr. and Mrs. Lussier. He had brought them to our home on a previous visit, and now he invited us to visit with him at their home. After making the necessary arrangements, we met him, Bill and I, and set out on one of the nicest two-day trips we've ever known.

Of course, I chided him unmercifully about being selfish and inconsiderate enough to get sick and throw us into such a panic with our First Saturday Mass. He assured me that it was Our Lady who had a hand in the whole thing. "I've been wanting you and Father Kennette to meet for a long time," he told me, "and she arranged the meeting for me." He told us that Father Kennette had been very much impressed with our dream of taking a group of invalids to the Shrines, particularly since I, myself, spent so much time in a wheelchair. Since Father Kennette conducted the perpetual Novena to St. Anne in St. Jean Baptiste, our pilgrimage undertaking was of great interest to him. St. Anne's Shrine in the lower church at St. Jean's was well known in New York, and the precious relic which was venerated there was the other half of the wristbone of St. Anne, which was the Major Relic at St. Anne de Beaupré. Father Kennette conducted pilgrimages to the Shrines, too, but because of limited time he, too, had been unable to take any seriously afflicted pilgrims with him. It was wonderful to know that he would be praying for the success of our pilgrimage at his Novena to St. Anne during the weeks to come.

During this time, Bill's mother was staying with his sister Kay in Washington, and while we were in Connecticut with Father Rinfret we mentioned this to him. "That's fine!" he said. "I have to go to Washington before going back to Canada, so you two keep me company on the journey and visit Bill's mother, too." When we called Kay to tell her of this proposed plan, she said she and her husband Ed would love to meet Father Rinfret, and we knew that such a visit would make Mother happy too, since we'd been telling her of our wonderful Canadian friends for a long time. So we spent another two days with Father, and he was completely forgiven for getting sick on us.

St. Anne, too, favored us with some very special visits around this time also. Father Levesque, one of the assistant pilgrimage directors, was in our area with one of the precious relics from the Shrine, so we had the privilege of having both Father and St. Anne at our home. A little later, we enjoyed our usual wonderful visit with Father Lefebvre, and it made us happy, indeed, to bring him to meet our new little grandson. This was Baby Don's first time to be blessed with a visit from St. Anne, but you can be sure it won't be his last!

# CHAPTER NINE

## *Sacred Heart Motif*

Late spring found us really up to our neck in plans. Our June and July pilgrimages were to be conducted much the same as in previous years, so they did not involve nearly so much time and effort as our special August pilgrimage for the handicapped. We were still short of funds, and since we had to arrange special transportation from the homes and hospitals to Grand Central Terminal, we were busy indeed. We would arrive at St. Joseph's in Montreal on Sunday, August 16th, where Father Bernard would have ample help waiting for us, and we would attend Mass and Communion and spend most of that day at the Oratory.

Late in the afternoon, we would go on to Our Lady of the Cape, where we would spend three days, and on Wednesday we would go on to St. Anne de Beaupré, where we would remain until after the Blessing of the Sick the following Sunday. Then, we would come directly home, arriving back in Grand Central Terminal early Monday morning. This meant

that we had scheduled eight pilgrimage Masses at
the Canadian Shrines. With our other groups, the
special Mass we attended on the morning of our
leaving gave our pilgrims nine Masses together —
a Novena of Masses. But with this special group,
we were leaving at night so that most of the hard
travelling would be done while our invalids slept. I
wanted them to have the graces of a Novena of
Masses  just as our other groups had, particularly
since we were leaving on a Holy Day of Obligation.
But the problem of getting all those wheelchairs in
and out of a parish church was overwhelming — in
fact, it was practically impossible. I don't even remember just when I began to think of having a
Mass in the waiting room of Grand Central Station,
immediately before we put our invalids into the Pullman berths, but the idea seemed such a simple solution to our problem  that it was with no misgivings
at all that I called the authorities at Grand Central
to discuss such a plan with them.

I was completely unprepared for the shocked
"Mass at Grand Central Terminal? Impossible!" that
met my request. "Why is it impossible? " I asked.
"Don't you realize what it means to these invalids
to be able to receive the grace of a *Novena* of
Masses, as well as the privilege of attending Mass
on a Holy Day of Obligation?" The fellow on the
phone told me that he was sorry, but such permission had never been granted, and if the authorities permitted a group of one faith such a special
privilege, it would have to grant equal privileges to
groups of other faiths. The argument seemed silly

to me, since they would only have to grant similar privileges under similar circumstances, and I was quite sure that they weren't going to be snowed under with people struggling to bring a group of cripples to the Canadian Shrines every day. But he was adamant, and told me that he was sorry, but he couldn't help me, and he hung up.

Indignantly, I wrote a letter to the authorities at the station, telling them that I thought it was truly a shame that Grand Central, the biggest station in the world, didn't have a heart to match, and how terrible it was that they would deny God's poor afflicted the solace of that special Mass. A day later, Mr. Holtman was sent by the railroad to discuss the matter further. He was so kind then, and in all the days to come. He was so very helpful with all our transportation problems, and when he saw how very much that particular Mass meant to me  he promised to discuss it further when he went back to the office. Later that evening, he called to tell me that he had gotten permission for the Mass from the authorities in the station, but that I, myself, would have to obtain ecclesiastical permission. Since the request was such an unusual one, he was a little doubtful that such permission would be granted, but I never doubted at all, since the Mass meant so much to my beloved pilgrim family.

Poor Father Kennette! I wonder that he doesn't rue the day he met me, I have called on him for help so many times since! Since I live in New Jersey, and Father is a priest in the Archdiocese of New

York, where the Mass would be said, I felt it would be easier for him to obtain the necessary permission, and I knew that with his great, kind heart, he would do all that he could to help us. After the greeting that I was getting used to hearing each time I mentioned it ("Mass in Grand Central Terminal?") Father said he'd be glad to call the Chancery Office and see what he could do. Later, he called back and said that he had spoken to his good friend Monsignor Dunellen, who took care of such matters. Monsignor told him that if we had been requesting this unusual privilege for a *morning* Mass he'd have been happy to grant it. But since we were leaving for Canada at night, and had requested permission for a Mass at 9 P.M., the matter was outside his jurisdiction. An evening Mass had never been said outside a parish church, and only Cardinal Spellman himself could grant such a privilege.

"I know how very much this Mass means to you, Mary," Father told me. "Why don't you write to the Cardinal and tell him all about it? He's a very saintly and understanding priest, and I'm sure he'll help you, if he can." Then he gently added, "If you *don't* get permission for the Mass, I'll come down myself, with some of the men from the parish, and carry your invalids into the evening Mass at St. Agnes's church. It's only a block away." I knew by these words that Father didn't think I had a chance of obtaining the permission I needed, and for the first time I too felt vague misgivings.

But with a prayer in my heart, I wrote to Cardinal Spellman, anyway. "Your Eminence," I wrote, "It is truly Divine Providence that makes you the only one who can give the necessary permission for this Mass I beg for God's beloved afflicted. You, who said Mass in many strange places and at strange times for men and women in the armed forces, surely would not have less done for those who serve in God's army of invalids." How can I describe the mixed emotions of humility and joy that were mine when I received the following letter less than a week later :

Dear Mrs. Varick :

In answer to your letter, I am pleased to grant you permission to have the Mass in Grand Central Terminal on the evening of your departure for the members of your pilgrimage and their friends. I would prefer that there be no publicity concerning this permission because a great many curiosity seekers might wish to be present at the Mass. I assume that Father Hornak will officiate.

Asking God to bless you and your pilgrimage, I am

Very sincerely yours in Christ,
† F. Cardinal Spellman
Archbishop of New York

From that moment on, with so great a blessing bestowed upon us, I knew that no matter how much work or heartache we encountered, our special pilgrimage would be a success. Each time a priest or some one else recommended an invalid who might like to join us, Bill and I went to meet them personally, and to tell them all our plans. While this entailed a great deal of running around, we both felt it was more than worthwhile, for it meant that we and our pilgrims would be old friends by the time we were leaving for Canada. This fact alone could add so much to the success of our pilgrimage.

In the meantime, we were still struggling with a financial shortage in our pilgrimage fund. Two wonderful things had happened in this respect. I received a check from Father Kennette for sixty dollars, with a letter explaining that he had told the people making his Novena to St. Anne, about our dream, and this money had been contributed by them in order to help us. They would like to meet us, the letter went on, and Father wondered if Bill and I would go over to St. Jean's the following Tuesday night. How often I've thanked Our Blessed Lady for bringing Father Kennette into our lives, even if she gave poor Father Rinfret a bad time in order to accomplish it.

When we went over to St. Jean's, Father introduced us to St. Anne's very good friends, and asked me to tell them in my own words why this pilgrimage was so important to me. While I chatter around here all day every day, this was my first poor attempt at speaking to a group, and with a vocabulary that is usually adequate for my needs I had great difficulty in finding words that could even begin to tell why I loved St. Anne so very much, and why I longed to bring other cripples to her Blessed Shrine of Beaupré. They were so kind and understanding, these friends of St. Anne's and Father Kennette's, and before I knew what was going on I had a lapful of contributions. In all, our pilgrimage fund was raised over two hundred and fifty dollars through the kindness of the good people of St. Jean's.

Then, too, Anna Mae Buckley of *The Advocate*, who had told our story in her paper the year before, wrote a follow-up article on our pilgrimage plan, and the wonderful readers of *The Advocate* had contributed over three hundred dollars to our fund. How truly grateful I am to all the good, kind people who did so much to help us with our great dream.

June was now at hand, and it was almost time for our first pilgrimage to leave for Canada, when we ran into a real problem. We had been hoping that Father Denman would be with us again, but just before we were to leave for the Shrines he was transferred to another parish and was unable to join us. With so little time, this created a problem indeed, and I frantically called one rectory and monastery after another, only to meet the same problem each time. At this time of the year, each parish was involved in graduation, weddings, retreats and vacation replacement, and since our pilgrimage plan would take them away from their parishes for two week-ends, we could find no priest who was free for that length of time. After knowing the special joy of having a priest of our own at the Shrines, I was sick at the thought of going without one. Since the June trip was dedicated to my beloved Sacred Heart, it was to Him I turned in supplication. "Wouldn't it be a terrible thing," I asked Him, "if the other groups had a chaplain of their own, and the one we have dedicated to You had to leave without one?" Only two days before we were leaving, the problem was still unsolved, and while I kept begging the Sacred Heart for help I was beginning to despair when I received a phone call from one of my brother's seminarian friends. "Mary," he said, "there is a missionary priest who has just arrived from Italy and has not yet been assigned to duty. While it is his first visit to our country and he might have a little difficulty with our language, he would be glad to be your pilgrimage chaplain if you want him to." Words tumbled over one another as I told Owen how happy and grateful I'd be to have him for our chaplain. "What is his name," I asked, "and to what order does he belong?" "He is Father Baiani," Owen told me, "and he belongs to the Sons of the Sacred Heart." How humble I felt as I realized that my best-loved Friend had so directly heard and answered my prayers once more. Later, when I met Father Baiani, I told him, "I begged the Sacred Heart for a priest, and he sent me one of His own sons."

Father answered me, "And I begged the Sacred Heart for a friend in this new country, and He sent me you, Mary." This added one more name to the long and impressive lists of special friends we have made in our effort to thank God for His goodness to us.

As it had been the year before, the June weather in Canada was ideal. Father Baiani was so impressed with the Shrines and loved every minute of the pilgrimage and every pilgrim in the group loved Father Baiani. Once more, we had three wheelchair pilgrims (reflecting my precious Trinity) and even more important, Fritz Hafemeister had flown all the way in from Tucson to join us in Mary's memory. How wonderful it was to be with him again! Mary's mother was with the four oldest children, and he had been boarding little Mary Lou, who was only nine months old when her mother died, in a nursery home. Fritz was not very happy with the plan, but it seemed best for all concerned, since Mary's mother was advanced in years and not too strong herself.

Sister Rita and Sister Gabriel were with us again, and once again were the best-loved pilgrims in the group. They had brought along four other sisters of another order, who were great friends of theirs. Mary and Ed McDonald, who were working so hard for our First Saturday Club, were also in the group (they are the parents of Sister Marian Eucharia, who'd been with us the year before) so in all I felt that the Sacred Heart had picked a pretty choice group of pilgrims for the group we had dedicated to Him.

I'd like to tell you about Marian Lentini, one of our wheel chair trio. While it was Marian's third time to go to Canada with us, it was her first pilgrimage as an invalid. Two years earlier, Marian joined our July pilgrimage and enjoyed it so very much that, at great personal sacrifice, she arranged to come back with us again in August of the same year. No one was more surprised at this than Marian, herself, who had always met the necessary requirements laid down by Holy Mother Church for her children, but who had never been overly spiritual, and will tell you quite frankly that she made the first trip because my niece Agnes, who was one of her best friends, told her what a wonderful time she could expect and how beautiful the Shrines were. So it was more or less as a tourist that Marian boarded the bus that first time. She was completely unprepared for the world of spiritual beauty and grace into which she was being plunged. We grew to be very close during the two pilgrimage trips, and in the strange and wonderful way of Divine Providence we had some long and serious talks. Marian, who loved dancing and activity of all sorts, found it hard to understand that I could be completely happy in affliction — that I had no wish at all to walk or dance. "Willingly carrying one's cross for love of God is a wonderful vocation in its own right," I told her, "and I feel so much closer to the Heart of my Jesus this way than I ever could if I could do all the things everyone else can. I truly believe that anyone who is blessed enough to understand the beauty of suffering for God as He did for us lives in a wonderful inner circle, close to His Sacred Heart."

When it came time for us to leave St. Anne de Beaupré for the second time, Marian found it even harder to leave than the first time. With tears

in her eyes, she told me that she felt she had received
a miracle all her own — the gift of understanding
and appreciating the beauty of our faith for the first
time. She told me that she would be counting the
days until she could come back with us again the
following year.

Less than a month later, Agnes called to tell
me that Marian had met with an accident. She had
fallen at work and had shattered her hip, and it
would be a long, long time (if ever) before she
would walk normally again. I immediately sent
Marian a telegram which said simply, "Congratulations and welcome to the inner circle." Truly a zany
message, which would have horrified most people,
but I was almost certain that, after all our long talks,
Marian would understand exactly what I meant. She
told me later that my message really changed her
life, and in the months that lay ahead she became
almost legendary in her smiling, uncomplaining acceptance of all the pain that was hers. The next
year, when we went to Canada again, Marian was
still in the hospital undergoing one difficult operation
after another. As we made plans for this year's
pilgrimages, she prayed so fervently that she would
be well enough to join us, even though she would
need a wheelchair. How happy we both were that
the doctor consented to her making the trip, and I
knew that, if it was God's holy will, Marian planned
to go along on each of the three pilgrimages. She
was working harder than anyone else on raising
funds for the afflicted, so that she could make it
possible for others to understand the lesson that she

had so painfully learned — that there is joy in affliction. When we finally reached the Shrine, and I watched Marian sitting quietly in her wheelchair, at the foot of St. Anne's Miraculous Statue, with peace and resignation so clearly written on her face, I marveled at the ways of God. How could Marian ever have guessed as she said farewell to the Shrine of St. Anne two years ago that when she returned she would be one of St. Anne's closest friends — an invalid?

The June pilgrimage was wonderful and spiritually so very rich, and so was July's. Once again, Divine Providence played a large part in the matter of our pilgrimage chaplain. These last few years, Father Bill had been with the July group, but he is the spiritual director of our First Saturday Club, and I was so very happy when he said that he would go with our special August pilgrimage instead. His lifelong devotion to the sick and afflicted and his gentle manner made him an ideal chaplain for our invalid group.

Do you remember me telling you about the winner of our pilgrimage trip for two, who was so happy to have won, that she was bringing a missionary priest as her guest? Well, Mrs. Hertz had chosen to make the trip she had won with our July group, and so we had her priest-guest as our chaplain. Father John Radaelli, a Consolata Father, is a wonderful priest, and we were all soon at perfect ease with him. He thought it very funny when I introduced him to Father Rinfret as "the chaplain we won in the raffle."

Again in July we had our trio of wheelchairs, and once again we were privileged to have some wonderful Sisters of Charity with us — Sister Elizabeth Anne and Sister Rose Genevieve. Marian was with us again, and so was most of our original pilgrimage group. I watched young Jimmy Fritzky doing so much to help our wheelchair pilgrims and marvelled at how the years were passing. He was only a little boy when he first came with us — I remember how thrilled I'd been when he served his first Masses at the Shrines!

I had a problem of my own that began to really worry me. For several months now I'd been suffering severe headaches, but in recent weeks they were developing into something more than mere headaches and I could no longer pass them off as a result of the added work of our extra busy pilgrimage season. I often suffered vertigo with them now, and occasionally I'd have fleeting moments of double vision or total darkness. I knew that the tremendous responsibility of our coming pilgrimage of the afflicted was really weighing very heavily on Bill, and I felt that adding the worry of my own health problem would be more than be could bear at this time. I begged God to see me through our August pilgrimage without any of my family knowing that I was not well. One day during the July stay at Our Lady of the Cape, when the headaches were much worse than usual, I confided in Father Rinfret, asking him to implore Our Lady's help in seeing me through the rest of the summer. I told him that I longed to be able to laugh and clown my way through the rest of the summer in my usual way so that not even those close to me would notice that anything was wrong. Our Lady heard his prayers, because even though the going was often rough, I did make the grade.

When we arrived home with our July group we had only three weeks left to complete the arrangements for our special August pilgrimage. We were still running badly in the red, and all of our hopes were on our final raffle. ( Here was our Trinity again — this would be the *third* raffle we held for our fund.) Catherine Engelbach, one of our First Saturday Club members, had contributed a very beautiful Infant of Prague to be raffled off, and in addition she had made several different outfits in breathtaking liturgical colors to go with the Infant. It was to be raffled off just three days before we were to leave for Canada, so our financial worry would exist until almost the last minute.

Art and Clare were joining us, with their children, on this trip, but instead of coming with us on the train they were driving up in their station wagon so that we would have it on hand for all the necessary running around during our week in Canada. Barbara, Darren's wonderful grandmother, had volunteered to be one of our nurses, and she was coming along on the train to be close to our invalids when they needed her. Another former pilgrim of ours, who was a registered nurse, had also volunteered her services. Her name is Marian Murphy, and she, too, planned to travel with the invalids. Dr. Lena Edwards, one of the truly great women doctors of our time, had volunteered her services, and was coming up from Washington to join us. So, while we might have financial worries, we were so rich in other privileges that I could not be grateful enough.

We had been expecting Yvonne to go with us again this August, and I was so terribly disappointed when I learned that she was not going because her father was unable to get his vacation at the time of our trip. Since we had grown to love Yvonne like a member of our own family, I was hurt and indignant to learn that her parents wouldn't let her go without them, because they felt that, with all the other invalids we planned to take, Yvonne would be too great a burden for us. I knew Yvonne had been looking forward to returning to the Shrines all winter, and so I wrote a letter to her parents, imploring them to let her come with us, even though they couldn't.

"I know how much you love her," I wrote in my letter, "and how you worry about her welfare. But as someone who has been crippled all my life, and who valued the privilege of making my own decisions so very much, please believe that this privilege is the greatest proof of your love you can give her. Won't you *please* let her come to Canada with us?" How kind and understanding they were to permit me to write such a presumptuous letter and not be angry with me. I felt truly humble when Yvonne's mother called me and said, "You're right, Mary; she should be permitted to make her own decisions, and while it wasn't very easy to accept at first, we've permitted her to make a decision far bigger than you anticipate. She is entering a religious order that accepts handicapped girls, and she is very, very happy. The name of the order? — Reparation to the Wounded Heart of Jesus!"

During these days of final preparation for our pilgrimage of the afflicted, we frequently saw Art and Clare MacMahon. In one of our conversations, I mentioned that Fritz Hafemeister was really unhappy about not being able to provide little Mary Lou with the home life that is so important during those early growing-up years. Not long afterward, Clare called and said, "Mary, Art and I have been talking about Mary Lou. It seems such a shame for Darren's crib and all his things to be standing idle when they could be doing so much good. If Fritz is willing, we'll take Mary Lou for as long as he wants us to." When Fritz accepted this heartwarming, generous offer, and flew in from Tucson to bring his baby to the MacMahons, it brought me such a strange kind of joy. I was just as sure that watching Clare and Art take care of her baby brought equal joy to Mary Hafemeister  as I had been that Mary had been waiting to welcome Darren home! And thinking of Darren and Mary and Yvonne filled me with such an unspeakable happiness, as I realized the incredible number of blessings God heaped on my pilgrim family. I had set out to organize pilgrim groups to thank God for His goodness to me, and each year the blessings He showered on us were so great and wonderful  that if I spent all my life trying to say "Thanks" I would never be grateful enough!

# CHAPTER TEN

## Our Afflicted Pilgrimage

The last week before our August pilgrimage was so full that I am sure I'll forget to tell you many important things about it, but I'll do the best I can. In addition to the Infant we were raffling off, we had containers for contributions in different parts of the city. Since this means of fund-raising is so overworked, most of the containers were disappointing, but a few of them were really great. There was the container which Tony and Margaret Klein returned with more than forty dollars in it. The Kleins have been faithful July pilgrims for many years, and I knew that the contents of that container was their own personal contributions. Then there was Carmela Volpe, who kept a container on the counter of her store, and at the end of each day added a "tithe of each day's wages" as the Bible suggested. With the help of her customers, she had succeeded in filling two containers and was working on the third when time ran out. And there were Irene Bennett and Jo Inverno and their friends, who stood for hours at various places with the containers and succeeded in turning in more than two hundred dollars to our fund. When all the containers were counted, and all the raffle money in, I almost broke down and cried. We had reached our goal! I can't even think of the raffles without thinking of Don and Kathleen Hilla. Although they have never been to Canada with us, they heard of our pilgrimage plans and joined our First Saturday group. Three times we held raffles and three times they sold over one hundred books! And on this final night of fund-raising they contributed a personal check of a hundred dollars. Oh, there were so many good and wonderful people who made it possible for us to reach our goal. I wish I could thank them all person-ally, but here in the pages of this book may I tell them all that they are so often in the prayers I say, each and every one of them, and I beg God over and over to bless them for the happiness they made possible for others who are less fortunate than they are.

During that week, Father Kennette called me, and told me of a priest who had been severely in-jured in a laboratory blast in Paris, and who was staying at the Monastery while undergoing plastic surgery in New York. He said that Father Erieau would like to go to Canada with us, and once again, I felt that God was being especially good to us. Among the other pilgrims who were going with us, was Sister Claire Cordis, a wonderful sister of Charity who had lost her sight in recent years. Here I had spent almost a year of my life working and planning this "vacation with God" for the handi-capped so that they might better understand the value of affliction and God had sent us these two special pilgrims, a blind nun and a crippled priest. If God would place the cross of affliction on the shoulders of those who had given Him their very lives, then surely those of us who were so much less deserving of His love must understand the merits of that cross, and accept our own affliction with better grace.

As I mentioned some time ago, we had to make special plans for the transportation of our afflicted to Grand Central Terminal. I don't know how we'd have ever managed if it hadn't been for the help of civil authorities in the towns and cities from which our pilgrims came. There was the Guttenberg police ambulance group, which brought Bill Cloupe and his wife in from their town; the Vailsburg Ambulance Corps, which brought Ed Sommerhalter in from Newark; The Madison Town Nurse, who brought Margaret McMahon in from there; the Jersey City Red Cross who used two station wagons to bring in the nine blind women from St. Joseph's Home; the Jersey City police who took care of Neil Gullikson, Howard Daniels, Sister Claire Cordis and her companion, Sister Regina, Margaret Murphy and Bill and me. The rest of our afflicted were fortunate enough to have some member of their family who could bring them to the station, but all that wonderful civic help made a very impressive sight as they arrived, one after another, in the special parking place which the New York Police and the station authorities had been good enough to reserve for us.

Once more, our Father Kennette was on hand to help us. It was he who brought all the physical requirements for our Mass down to Grand Central. The vestments, hosts, candlesticks and all came from St. Jean's and when I tried to thank Father for all this, he told me that he considered it a privilege to have a part in so great a dream. He had even arranged for the confessions of our invalids to be heard.

The happiness that was mine as that strange and wonderful Mass began is indescribable, but I am sure that the song in my heart must have been heard a mile away. As our own dear Father Bill began the Mass, the only prayer that I seemed able to say was "Thank You, my Jesus, thank You!" over and over again. It was a High Mass and my brothers and their seminarian friends chanted it. I was sure that those looking down from Heaven to that beautiful and unusual scene in the middle of the largest railroad station in the world must have been just as moved as we were. And a little later, when I held my Jesus close to my heart in the Blessed Sacrament, I thanked Him once more for making all this possible, and implored Him to watch over and protect these dear invalids of His during the strenuous days ahead of us.

After Mass, the Union News Company served all of our group coffee and doughnuts, a wonderful, kind act for which I was so very grateful. And after a real hectic half-hour or so, we were all aboard our reserved railroad cars, and my dream was fast becoming a reality.

We arrived in Montreal Sunday morning to find Father Bernard of St. Joseph's Oratory waiting for us with station wagons and seminarians. I had arranged to have two buses waiting for the rest of us to take us first to the Oratory and later on to Our Lady of the Cape. It was raining when we arrived, but this was not enough to dampen the spirits of our group, and it cleared up in a little while.

Father Bernard's warm, sincere welcome to St. Joseph's was unforgettable, and throughout the entire day he worked tirelessly to see that our group was well taken care of. After Mass, we went to the cafeteria to eat, and then Father took our group all through the Oratory and the Shrine grounds. It was strange that this severely handicapped group got to see more of St. Joseph's than I myself had ever seen, and I'll never be grateful enough to Father Bernard for all that he did for us. Before leaving for the Cape, Father Bernard arranged for Benediction and the individual blessing of the sick, and it was our own Father Bill who held our blessed Lord in the Monstrance over each one of us as he gave us his blessing.

Father Frotton, the new young curate in our own parish, knew how desperately we needed help with our large group of invalids, and he arranged to take his vacation so that he and his brother, Peter, could join us with his station wagon. The Mac-Mahons had joined us, too, that morning, and we were now eighty-three in number. With the two station wagons to transport the invalids who could not travel by bus, and two buses to take the rest of us, we were quite a caravan as we set out for Our Lady of the Cape. I remember thinking of a funny little numerical coincidence at that time. There were four vehicles in our group, and our youngest pilgrim, little Claire Cassidy, was four years old. There were eighty-three of us in the group, and our oldest pilgrim, Mary Albright, from St. Joseph's Home for The Blind, was eighty-three years old.

We arrived at Our Lady of the Cape about seven o'clock and when we pulled up to the door of the Pilgrim's House to find all the Oblate Sisters whom we had grown to love so much through the years waiting for us, as well as St. John's Ambulance Corps who were waiting to help us, it was almost more than I could bear. The full realization of the fantastic thing we had done sank in as I watched our stretcher cases and wheelchair cases and the blind being helped into the Pilgrim's House, and I broke down and cried like a baby. Truly, I am God's own fool — and He is so very, very good to me!

Father Rinfret had been sitting on the porch of the Pilgrim's House for hours, waiting to welcome us, but we arrived quite a bit later than we expected to, and he had been called away to take care of an important matter just a few moments before we arrived. As soon as he heard we were there, he hurried back to greet us, and there was an enthusiastic burst of noise as our group welcomed this dear, old friend. You see, quite a few of us knew him well, either from previous pilgrimages or his frequent visits to our home in the States.

By the way, I forgot to tell you something about my own family. All year long, I had been begging them to try to join us, no matter how great the sacrifice, since our invalids were going to need so much help getting dressed and eating and getting around the Shrines. I knew that they all wanted to help; they had all worked so hard on the fund-raising detail, but never in my wildest dreams did I think they'd be able to give us so much help with the actual pilgrimage. There was my oldest brother, Jim, and his wife Helen, with six of their eight children. My second brother, Joe, and his wife, Dot, were with us, too. Then there was Ed, who brought Bill and me on that first wonderful trip to St. Anne de Beaupré so long ago. And last, but far from least, were my two seminarian brothers, Frank and Jack, and two of their classmates, Lou and Owen. Since my only sister, Rose, has several small children at home, she was unable to be with us, but her daughter Joan, who is studying to be a sister of Charity, was with us. Of course, so were our own children, who had lived a whole year right in the shadow of this dream as we worked to make it come true. My dear mother, who had been with us during two other pilgrimage years, is so soft-hearted and distressed at the sight of great suffering that I knew spending nine days with our seriously handicapped pilgrims (there were thirty-seven of them ) would be too great an ordeal for her, and I was relieved when she herself said that she thought it would be wiser not to make the trip with us. But I knew that we could count on her thoughts and prayers every day, and I drew much comfort and courage from that knowledge.

By ten o'clock or so, our pilgrim family had been fed and tucked comfortably into bed. All of us were exhausted, since we had been travelling since the night before. But I could not retire until I had taken care of one more very important matter. I asked Estelle Clavette, who was in charge of the Pilgrim's House, and a very dear personal friend, if she would take me over to the Shrine, as I had something I must do before going to bed. Bill was still busy, taking care of last-minute details, so Estelle and I made the trip to the Shrine by ourselves. As we walked along through the lovely, familiar grounds, I was so afraid that I might wake up and find this all a wonderful dream. We entered the Shrine, and she pushed my wheelchair to the altar rail directly in front of the Miraculous Statue of Our Lady. I slid to my knees, and as the grateful tears slipped quietly down my cheeks I was aware that Father Rinfret had come in and was kneeling beside me. I handed him the crumpled Canadian dollar I had been holding in my hand — yes, it was the one he had given me for our pilgrimage fund, many months ago — and asked him if he would light a candle at Our Lady's feet, as I had promised her I would if I ever succeeded in reaching her Shrine with my invalid family.

Father lit the candle and knelt beside me again. Estelle was kneeling on the other side of me. "Would you like to say three 'Hail Mary's' in thanksgiving?"

he asked, and gratefully, I nodded, "Yes." Three of us, who loved Our Lady so much, saying three "Hail Mary's" in gratitude — my blessed Trinity again! I had begged the Blessed Trinity so long and so hard to make this pilgrimage possible, but it was not until the next morning, when Father Rinfret mentioned that he was planning the individual blessing of the sick for our group before we left, that I realized how much They had answered my prayers. They had already received such a blessing at St. Joseph's Oratory, and they would definitely receive another one at St. Anne de Beaupré on Shut-ins' Day, so with the one Father mentioned at Our Lady of the Cape, I'm sure they would have received a privilege no other group had received before them — three individual blessings of the sick, with the Blessed Sacrament, at three wonderful Shrines. To go on with our blessings of three, we were accompanied by three priests, Father Bill, Father Erieau and Father Frotton. We had with us three sub-deacons, my brother Jack and Lou and Owen. There were three of our group in the medical profession, Dr. Edwards, and our nurses, Barbara MacMahon and Marian Murphy. There were also three professed religious, Sister Claire Cordis and Sister Regina and Brother Celestine of Graymoor. There were three girls aspiring to vocations as Sisters of Charity, Joan, Carol Coneys and my Mary, and three boys who hope some day to serve God as brothers, Jim Garrison, Doug Detroy and my Jim. Could anyone doubt that my prayers had been heard?

Whenever we stay at the Cape, after the candle-light procession is over, some of us usually meet Father Rinfret in the restaurant on the riverside for a snack and some fun. Father and his friends will sing some of their French songs for us and some of our group sing our songs for them. There is always much laughter and fun, and once, when I was worried that such behavior wasn't proper on the Shrine grounds, I wrote Father Rinfret a letter, asking him to tell us, honestly, if we are ever out of order. "You know how much we love Our Lady," I wrote, "and with what reverence and love our pilgrimages are planned. I would never want our group to be disrespectful in any way." I still treasure his answer to this day. "Even Our Lady loves to laugh," Father wrote, "so each year, she waits to take her vacation with you, Mary."

This special pilgrimage was to be no exception, and when Father and I were talking about getting together socially I asked him if he'd come to the sitting room of the Pilgrim's House after the procession, since it would be pretty difficult to move all our wheelchairs and blind to the restaurant on the riverside. He agreed, and that evening turned out to be an unforgettable one. The seminarians sang for us, and Father Rinfret and some of St. John's Ambulance Corps sang for us, Brother Celestine played the piano and the blind women sang and recited for us, too. But the highlight of the evening came when Father asked our Barbara if she'd like to play the mirror game with him. Barbara said she'd like to, but she didn't know how and Father said he'd be glad to show her how. (Poor Barbara didn't realize that the fact that she *didn't* know the mirror game made her a perfect candidate!)

Father brought in a small table and a candle. He lit the candle, put out the overhead lights and sat on one side of the table and instructed Barbara to sit opposite him. "Now I'm supposed to be a young lady, sitting at my dressing table, putting on my make-up, and you are my reflection in the mirror." he told her. "Since you *are* my reflection, the point of the game is that you must do every single thing I do." He turned to all the pilgrims and said, "Your job is to watch her, and see if she misses anything at all."

He then said, "First, we'll put on our hats," and he handed her a pie plate just like the one he held in his own hand, and they both balanced them on their heads. "Now for our cold cream," he continued, as he made motions of one smearing cold cream all over her face. "Oops, our hats are slipping, and each time they do, we must straighten them again," he instructed and from then on, they went through the most frantic routine of straightening their hats and rubbing cold cream on their faces. Barbara, with all the bubbling enthusiasm of a sixteen-year old, rubbed twice as hard as Father Rinfret and straightened her hat with equal vigor. It only took the group in the room a few minutes to grasp the fact of which Barbara was completely unaware in the candlelight. *Her* pie plate was covered with lamp black and Father's was not. Therefore, each time she straightened her hat, and applied her cold cream, she was blackening her own face. In less time than it takes to tell, she had done such a fantastic job on herself that Aunt Jemima would have been proud to claim her. Everyone in the room was howling with glee, and Barbara, herself, was laughing hilariously, and it *was* funny watching the two of them at opposite ends of the table mimicking each other, even without the lamp black. But finally I couldn't bear it any more, and told Barbara to look in a real mirror. It is at moments like these that mothers are so proud of their children. Some sixteen-year old girls would have been horrified at being made such a spectacle of, but I was sure that I could count on Barbara's sense of humor and the fact that she is such a good sport. One look in the mirror and she collapsed in an hysterical heap of laughter. Yes, in fairness to Father Rinfret, I have to confess that I *did* know how the mirror game was played, and when Father asked me if I thought Barbara would mind such a joke being played on her, I assured him that she wouldn't. "All of the Varicks have learned to laugh at themselves," I boasted. How I love Barbara for not letting me down!

Each day, Father Erieau had been quietly saying his Masses on a side altar, privately, because he was self-conscious of his poor disfigured hands and face. With our priests and sub-deacons and organist (Lou played the organ at the seminary) and our choir (all the seminarians with us were members of Darlington's choir and sang our Masses each day) and our acolytes (the boys who aspire to the brotherhood) our group was in a position to have Solemn High Masses every day without needing any help from anyone outside our group. It was an incredible thing, and the priests at each of the Shrines commented on it, saying that they had never seen such a group before. One day, I asked Father Erieau if he would be deacon at the next day's solemn High Mass. He hesitated, because the idea was such a new one, and he told me that he doubted if he could manage the book and censer, etc. I told him I was sure that something could be worked out, with the seminarians around to help, and I asked him to think about it during the day. "It would mean so very much to us," I told him, "to have you there on God's altar representing all of us, God's own afflicted." Later that day, he told me that he would be deacon at the next day's Solemn High Mass, and I was very happy. But I was in for such a surprise, and so rich a spiritual blessing, that I ache with my own inability to do this precious moment justice. What words could? After Mass the following day, Father Rinfret announced that Benediction and blessing of the sick would follow immediately. It was *Father Erieau* who said Benediction, and when he came down into the church, holding my Jesus in his poor crippled hands, to bless each one of us in our wheelchairs and pews, I was so moved that I almost choked with emotion. I knew from the sound of soft sobbing in the pews behind me that everyone else had been equally touched. Father

Erieau, in his own affliction, brought our crucified Christ closer to us than any other priest could possibly have done.

It was soon time for us to go on to St. Anne de Beaupré, and the moment which, for me, was always the highlight of each pilgrimage — the moment when St. Anne, through the beautiful pilgrim bells, would ring out her warm welcome as we entered her Basilica. One would think that after all the times I had heard them (this was the fifteenth pilgrimage for Bill and me ) I would have grown used to them by now. But I have never been able to go up the aisle of the Basilica without weeping, remembering my first entrance to this heavenly place, when I was so close to death. And each time, I remember again how inconceivably great is my debt of gratitude to God and Good St. Anne.

It is only natural that our arrival at St. Anne's this time, with all her beloved invalids, should be the most rewarding of all. As I glanced down the long row of wheelchairs, lined up near the altar rail, and then looked up into the beloved face of the Grandmother of Jesus, I could scarcely see through the mist of grateful tears that filled my eyes. The bells subsided into silence, and the dear, familiar voice of Father Lefebvre bid us welcome. As he looked down at me from the pulpit, I knew that, because of our years of close friendship, he knew what this precious moment meant to me.

After saying "Hello " to Saint Anne, we proceeded to get our pilgrim family settled in their rooms. We had made reservations for our seriously afflicted in rooms on the first floor of the Hotel Regina, which is the closest accommodations to the Shrine itself. The rest of us were a little further down the road at the Twin Towers Motel, and there were so many of us that we had the entire motel to ourselves. I had worked for this dream, with the earnest prayer that these special friends of God's would better understand the affliction that was theirs, and that they would think, too, of all the good things He had given them.

I can't tell you what it meant to me to hear all our blind pilgrims, when they heard the commotion of our wheelchairs and stretchers getting settled, say, "Oh, those poor people, who can't walk. Thank God that we have the use of our feet!" And our wheelchair pilgrims would watch the blind being led around and murmur, "Oh, how hard it must be to be blind. Thank God we can see!" Oh, what a rich reward for all our months of work!

On our second night at St. Anne's a very wonderful thing happened. Bishop Lussier, of Alberta, who had been Pilgrimage Director the first year that Bill and Bud and I came here, made a brief visit to the Shrine, and the unexpected joy of seeing him again was so wonderful that I could not help but feel that it was Good St. Anne's own doing. He said the evening Mass, and afterward came out to talk to us. I introduced him to all our special pilgrims, and he was so kind and gracious to each of them as he blessed them and let each one kiss his ring. He came back to me and said, "It is such a wonderful group, Mary. You must be truly happy."

"I am, Your Excellency, and this pilgrimage took a Novena of my life to achieve." It was nine years ago that I sat in the Basilica, and sobbed to Father Lussier, "I don't want to walk like other people. I can love and serve God so much better as a cripple."

Some of our invalids had found the hundred-mile trip from St. Joseph's to the Cape very difficult by bus, and the second hundred-mile jaunt from the Cape to St. Anne's had been equally difficult for them. The more I thought about the two hundred miles that had to be travelled straight through back to Montreal where we were to meet our Pullman cars, the more I worried, and finally I decided that it would actually be too difficult for them to bear. I decided to call Grand Central in New York and see if I could have our railroad cars moved up to Quebec, which was only a little more than twenty miles from the Shrine of St. Anne de Beaupré. They would easily be able to travel that far by bus, and once they were settled on the train in Quebec they would not have to be moved again until they reached New York.

This would be a costly move indeed, one for which we had not planned, but I did not see how it could be avoided, since the health and comfort of our invalids was the most important thing to be considered. How I thanked God for the wisdom and thoughtfulness of Father Rinfret, who knew so much more about travelling expenses and unforeseen incidents than I did. It was he who insisted I hold on to the money with which I was to pay for our reservations at the Cape until we were safely home. "You can always send it later," he told me, "and this way you'll be sure to have money for any emergency." How grateful I was to him as I made definite plans with the railroad to have the cars brought to Quebec. I could not have done so without his money, and I can't imagine how our group could have stood the grueling, two-hundred-mile bus ride to Montreal. It thrilled me to be able to make this change in plan, but there was still more difficulty lying ahead. There were only two trains leaving Montreal for New York on that Sunday, and if we were to wait for the special blessing of the sick that afternoon our special cars would get out of Quebec too late to make connections with the main line train. Therefore, the railroad official told me we would have to plan on leaving in time to make the earlier train, which meant that we had to leave the Shrine *before* the blessing of the sick.

"Oh, no," I wailed, "You don't understand. I've given a whole year of my life to this pilgrimage, and one of the most important parts of our planning — as a matter of fact, the *main* part of our planning was to be here for this special blessing. You *couldn't* ask me to take my poor afflicted pilgrims away before it, when the Bishop himself is going to bless each one of them individually with the Blessed Sacrament in the Monstrance!"

"I'm sorry, lady, but if you were to stay for

that blessing, we'd have to hold up our mainline train twenty minutes or more."

"What is twenty minutes in comparison to a year of unbelievable work and sacrifice? Isn't there *anyone* you can talk to about it?" In a tone of pained resignation, he sighed, "I'll see what I can do about it, and call you back tomorrow morning. But remember," he admonished, before hanging up, "I'm not *promising* you anything!"

That evening when I was in the Basilica for the evening Mass I looked up at St. Anne and whispered, "You *couldn't* permit them to make us take your friends away before that special blessing, could you, dear St. Anne?" Did I detect a wee smile playing about the corner of her eyes? I'm almost sure I did! In fact, I wasn't even too surprised the next morning when the railroad official called to say that he and some other officials had talked it over, and because of the very unusual circumstances, had agreed to hold the mainline train for us so that we *could* attend the blessing. I thanked him fervently, and even more fervently thanked Good St. Anne, and I can still see the incredulous look on the faces of our group when I told them that the train was actually being held up in Montreal so that we could receive this very special blessing. I remembered too the words of my dearest Friend "Ask and you shall receive!" I was just beginning to understand that powerful advice.

Each precious moment of these pilgrimage days seemed to be flying by. Before we knew it, Sunday was upon us. What a hectic day that was!

Father Lefebvre had very kindly arranged to have all our luggage brought into the railroad station in Quebec, and while the blessing of the sick was not until three in the afternoon we first had to have our group checked out of both the Hotel Regina and Twin Towers. This was the morning of our ninth Pilgrimage Mass. As I watched Father Bill saying it on the main altar of the Basilica, I wondered what I could possibly say to my God in thanksgiving. My dream was complete — my pilgrim family had their Novena of Masses for which I had fought so hard. I looked along the row of wheelchairs and into the faces of the blind, and I could clearly see there a peace and serenity that had not been there before. And overwhelmed with the full impact of the complete realization of my dream I could find *no* words at all to whisper to my God. At Communion time, I held Him so close, mute and humble with gratitude, and all that I could offer Him in exchange for all He had given me was a weak and shaky heart, so full of love and thanksgiving that I could scarcely breathe. I knew He understood my silence, and I knew, too, that He understood how much I meant the prayer I had whispered to Him so many times in these last years of my life: "Oh, Lord that I might live to be just a humble instrument of Your Love!"

Breakfast, packing and loading all the luggage, last-minute checkout, lunch, and it was time for our final visit to the Basilica. The buses which were to take us to Quebec would pick us up right on the Shrine grounds, immediately after the Blessing of the Sick.

As the breathtaking beauty of the Procession of the Sick began, with only the clergy and the invalids taking part, how I wished that the railroad officials who had made it possible for us to be here could have seen it. It would have been all the thanks they ever needed for their great kindness to us, and I knew that they'd have considered the inconvenience of holding up their mainline train well worthwhile. It was held outdoors, through the park in front of the Basilica, and after the procession all the invalids were lined up around the park while the bishop went to each one of them and blessed them individually with the Monstrance. As my Jesus was held momentarily above my own head, I implored Him to bless everyone who had even the tiniest part in making this wonderful pilgrimage possible — and I asked Him especially to bless the railroad officials!

Father Lefebvre came to the buses with us to add his personal farewell and blessing as we left. Looking back at St. Anne's Basilica, which was so very dear to me, I told Father Lefebvre, "It's up to her now, Father. If it is God's Holy Will, with her help, I'll bring them back to her again next year."

"It is one of the most beautiful, perfect groups I have ever seen in all my years at the Shrine," Father said, "and I am sure that she'll help you bring them back!"

When we were finally settled on the train, homeward bound, I could not stop thinking of how hard every single person who was not afflicted had worked from morning until late at night, looking after the welfare and comfort of our invalids. Dr. Edwards and Barbara MacMahon and Marian Murphy had been tireless in their labor of love, and even the youngest children in the group were always looking for some kind little thing that they could do for these special friends of God's. Oh, it had been a physically exhausting nine days, but I knew that every single one of us, afflicted *or* well, was richer for it. And in the strange ways of God, I almost was convinced that the well pilgrims, for all their unselfish and unceasing work, had derived even more grace from the pilgrimage than the invalids — all they could talk about was volunteering their services again next year! We arrived back in Grand Central Terminal Monday morning to find our wonderful civic help waiting to bring our pilgrims back to their homes. Yes, the ambulances and police cars were all there, and there was only a little mix-up. Through some misunderstanding, the Jersey City Red Cross station wagons were unable to be there to bring the blind back to St. Joseph's, but the New York City Red Cross took over for them, and I was so very grateful. As I sat in my own home a little later that morning, it all seemed like a fantastic dream — could anything so wonderful really have happened? The peace of soul and joy of heart that was mine told me that it had!

# CHAPTER ELEVEN

## *Light from Darkness*

Now it was time, as I had promised, to look into the matter of my own health. Bill was not yet aware of the constant, terrible headaches which plagued every moment of my waking hours, but he knew that I was close to physical exhaustion. Father Rinfret had suggested, several times, that after the group was safely back in their own homes I return to the quiet serenity of the Cape, as his guest, for a week or so. During the first few days at home, Bill pushed that suggestion, since he had to return to work anyway, and the Saturday after our return with the group he brought me to Newark Airport and put me on a plane back to Canada. Since three things could be accomplished by my making this return trip it was not too hard to convince me. (Yes, three again!) I could get the rest I needed so badly, and which I couldn't get at home, with the phone ringing from morning until late at night, with people wanting to hear all about our wonderful pilgrimage; I could straighten out some necessary details on next year's pilgrimage plans as well as talk to Father Rinfret about plans to clear up the bill I owed at the Cape (remember, I had spent their money to bring the railroad cars to Quebec? We were really in the red!) and I knew that Father Rinfret could make an appointment with the doctor near the Shrine so that I could find out just how serious my problem was before alarming my loved ones.

This was my first flying experience and I loved every minute of it. It had taken us over nine hours to reach Montreal by train, the plane made it in one hour and ten minutes. As the plane soared along and I looked out at the white clouds just beneath us, I could imagine being lulled to sleep in a soft feather bed, so gentle was the motion of the plane. What a wonderful way this would be to bring our invalids to Canada, I mused. It would cut their travelling time to a fraction, and the ride was far more smooth than any car, bus or train I had ever ridden in. Almost unconsciously, I found myself telling God, "With Your help, this is the way we'll come next year!"

Father Rinfret had told me that he'd have someone waiting at the airport to meet me. As the plane circled the airport, I looked down and could hardly keep from chuckling aloud at the sight that met my eyes. There was Jean Normandin, the Shrine's photographer and our very dear friend, sitting on the field in the wheelchair he'd brought down from the Cape for me, calmly watching my plane come in. Oh, how rich and blessed I am in precious friendships. That Father Rinfret and Jean would do so much to make this holiday possible for me almost filled me with tears. You see, the airport was over a hundred miles from the Shrine, yet Father had sent Jean in, with his own (Father's) car, to meet me at the airport. That was the beginning of one of the most perfect weeks of my life. Only one thing could have made it more perfect — I missed my Bill.

I could almost write a book on just the fun I had at the Pilgrim's House. I loved each and everyone of those Oblate Sisters, and since I had quite a reputation for my silly sense of humor the week was full of all sorts of practical jokes. When I ordered spaghetti for supper that night, I was served a few strands of uncooked spaghetti with a whole clove of garlic on top. The next morning, my breakfast consisted of an uncooked egg, some raw bacon and tea, served in an eggcup. Each of these incidents brought peals of laughter from all of us, and the meal that followed was always an especially wonderful peace offering.

Each day was full of unbelievable happiness as I attended several of the Masses, joined in each evening's candlelight procession, or just sat and hungrily drank in the loveliness of our Lady's Shrine. It was the first time I had ever been able to relax so — it was the first time I'd ever been here alone, without the responsibility of a pilgrimage group. I often visited Father Rinfret in his office, and we had straightened out our plans for next year. He had reassured me concerning our bill, and I knew that, somehow, God would make it possible to take care of this debt in the very near future.

During the week, Jean had been my constant mealtime companion. Each meal was a joy in itself, for Jean has a fabulous sense of humor, and we laughed and giggled our way through each mealtime. But we had some wonderful, serious talks and I got to know, better than ever, what a truly fine fellow Jean is, and how very much he loves Our Lady. All the Oblates were wonderful to me, but it was Louise who was always nearby, waiting to do anything she could to help me, and taking me any place at all that I wanted to go. We went to Mass each morning together, and each night she was there to bring me to the candelight procession. How I grew to love her through those happy days, and how grateful I am for all her kindness to me.

Father Rinfret made the appointment with a doctor in Three Rivers, as I had asked him to, and it was Louise and Jean who took me there. It took only a few moments of the examination for me to realize that the doctor thought I had a serious problem, indeed. I knew without his telling me that the symptoms (constant headache, vertigo, impaired vision and loss of balance ) *could* indicate a brain tumor. He advised me to go into the hospital immediately for further tests, but I told him that I would be leaving for home in a few more days, and that I would prefer to enter the hospital at home, close to my family.

That night, as I sat close to the Miraculous Statue of Our Lady, I told her that I was completely resigned to the suffering and possible death that the future might hold for me, and that I would willingly offer whatever the coming days might bring, to her Divine Son, for all the blessings He had given me. Later, as I circled the grounds during the candle-light procession, and listened to the beautiful promises of Fatima as that scene was enacted on the island, I hungrily stored one precious scene after another into my treasury of memories. Would I ever see them all again, I wondered? How could I know that it was blindness, not death, that might make this my last precious view of this place I loved so much?

During the days of my visit, Father Rinfret and I often talked of our wonderful pilgrimage for the afflicted, and Father asked if I would write an article regarding it, while I was there, so that it could be published in the Annals. A day or so before I left, I handed him the following article :

### Dreams *Do* Come True

It was quiet and peaceful in an unearthly way, and the song in my heart blended with the gentle "Aves" of the Perpetual Rosary Group. I did not need to have Our Lady open her eyes to know that she was looking down at that same heart, overflowing with gratitude. It might have been a dream that I had dreamed many times, were it not for the hard reality of cold marble pressing against knees not used to kneeling. Sitting in a wheelchair at her feet seemed far too easy a way to say "Thanks" for all the graces that were ours, and so I had managed to slide from my wheelchair to my knees before Our Lady's Miraculous Statue.

There were no formal prayers of thanks — I knew that the crumpled Canadian dollar clutched tight in my hand spoke more eloquently to my Heavenly Mother than any words could. I'd had it almost a year; it had been one of the first contributions to our pilgrimage fund. Even more important, it had been donated by one of Our Lady's best loved friends, and so it had become a symbol of love to me. From the beginning, I had vowed that if God gave us the grace to bring a group of invalids to the Cape, the first thing I would do would be to take that dollar to Our Lady's Shrine and light a candle in thanksgiving.

Oh, if that dollar could talk, what stories it would tell! Who could count the times I took it from its hiding place during the long cold months of winter? It could tell of tears of disappointment and discouragement, when our dream seemed beyond reach. It could tell of moments of elation, when things seemed to be going almost too well. Yes, if inanimate things could speak, that dollar could tell of a year of love and effort, joy and sacrifice known to very few.

But more than all of this, I wish it could tell you why our dream was born. God's greatest gift to me is the ability to understand that, in His eyes, suffering has great value, because it was through the medium of suffering that His Divine Son redeemed the world. For this reason, I've always considered the affliction that is mine a rare and special privilege. How I've yearned to share that conviction with other invalids, particularly those sentenced to imprisonment within the four lonely walls of a shut-in's room. How could I reach them to tell them of the advantage of belonging to God's beloved army of sufferers, how could any poor words of mine convince them that resting quietly in the gentle hands of Jesus, in perfect submission to His Holy Will, could bring them an abundance of joy that would make the treasures of the world seem dull by comparison?

At last I found the answer. If they could be brought to the beautiful Canadian Shrines and shown how warmly they were received, it would be easy to convince them that they held an even more important place in the heart of God. And so it began — the monumental task of planning and raising funds for the pilgrimage for the afflicted. Our dream was to take every invalid who wished to join us, regardless of the severity of his affliction or his financial status. Do you wonder that I looked back, so many times, at that first precious, significant dollar?

Well the details of the year in between would be too long and tedious a story for anyone to read. Let us just say that each worried moment, each heartache we knew, each fear of failure we suffered were more than rewarded a few short weeks ago, when our pilgrimage of invalids arrived at Our

Lady's Shrine. And after our pilgrims were tucked safely into bed, with the wonder of Our Lady's love surrounding them, and the warmth of her hymns still echoing in their hearts, I set out to do the thing I had dreamed of doing more times than I could count — to light that candle in thanksgiving.

For me, this was one of the most precious moments of all, in a week overflowing with blessings. I had kept my promise — that Canadian dollar was back at the Shrine, and when the candle was lighted, there were three of us kneeling there in thanksgiving. Looking down, Our Lady must have been reminded of another trio that knelt before her a long time ago, even though our petitions were different. There was Estelle Clavette, gentle, gracious hostess of the Pilgrim's House, who brings to Our Lady's Home at the Shrine the same warmth and understanding one would expect to find in a simple home in Nazareth many centuries ago. Then, there was Father Rinfret, whose very name stirs the wonder of Our Lady's love in so many, many hearts. And in the center, kneeling in almost the same spot occupied by Pierre Lacroix on that blessed night when Our Lady opened her eyes, was a cripple. How I begged her to grant our pilgrims the special favor for which we had worked so hard to bring them to her. "Oh, Mary," I pleaded, "Grant them the privilege of understanding the grace of *not* being cured, so that their whole lives may become an act of love and reparation to the wounded Heart of your Divine Son. Help them to sanctify their sufferings by letting them know that perfect resignation to His Holy Will assures them of eternal happiness." No, it was not necessary for her to open her eyes to let me know she heard my plea. The peace that flooded my soul was all the answer I needed.

During this visit of mine, there was for me a special source of great spiritual joy. When we were here with our groups, we always had our own Masses, said by our pilgrimage chaplain, and during the days of the pilgrimage season, when all the responsibility of the Shrine activities was his, Father Rinfret was so very busy that, as a rule, he said his own Mass, each day, early in the morning in the chapel at the Monastery. While I had attended his Masses when he was visiting in the United States, I had never attended a Mass of his at the Shrine. I mentioned this to him early in the week of my visit, and during the week he arranged to say an early Mass on the main altar (and I had the privilege of attending them) three times — yes, my Trinity again! It was during these Masses that I realized fully how rich I was indeed to have "another Christ" like this for my friend, and it was the joy these Masses brought me and the full knowledge of what my own future might hold that prompted me to write the following poem :

## CONSECRATION

To Father Rinfret, in humblest thanks for the precious moment in his Mass, when he brought God to me, and me to God.

In Host held high, what do I see?
My Jesus, Who was born for me.
Sweet, gentle Babe, in manger bare.
Oh, how I wish that I'd been there
To hold Him close, to kiss His toes,
To watch o'er Him, in sweet repose.
In Host held high, what do I see?
My Jesus, Who has lived for me.
Who walked the earth so men might learn
Just how His Sacred Heart did Yearn
To teach of love without an end,
To be to man, his dearest Friend.
In Host held high, what do I see?
My Jesus, Who has died for me.
O, Spotless Host, turned crimson red
With blood the Lamb of God has shed.
His Body torn by vicious whips,
Bitter gall upon His lips.
O. Jesus, Jesus, hear my cry!
With all my love, I long to try
To make of my heart, three things for You.
Manger, temple — gibbet, too.
Dearest Love, Who died for me
I long to die, with love, for Thee!

And thus it was that my wonderful week at
the Cape ended. I gave Father the poem just as I
was leaving, and before Jean drove me back to the
airport to take a plane home I went into the Shrine
to say "Farewell" to Our Lady. I can't describe all
the emotions I felt — would I ever kneel here again
(yes, I was kneeling in the same spot I knelt in the

night our thanksgiving candle was lit) — only God knew! Father Rinfret knelt on one side of me and Jean on the other. "Would you like to say three Hail Mary's?" Father asked, and again I nodded, "Yes." The three of us kneeling there, saying those three  Hail Mary's  is the last precious jewel in my treasury of memories of my visit to the Shrine.

I got home on Friday night, just in time to complete the last details for our First Saturday Mass and Breakfast. Yes, we've been keeping our promise to bring our invalid group to Mass, Communion and a little social gathering each month. The First Saturday before we left for Canada we had gone to the Shrine of St. Anne in New York, and Father Kennette had said our Mass. This seemed so very fitting, for it gave us a chance to beg St. Anne's help, in a special way, for the job that lay ahead. Next month  (October) we plan to go to the Monastery of the Sons of the Sacred Heart, where Father Baiani will say our Mass. But September's Mass, which was to be said the day after my return from Canada, was a special one of thanksgiving — a Solemn High Mass in Sacred Heart Cathedral in our own arch-diocese of Newark. Father Bill was saying the Mass, and my own brother  Jack  was the subdeacon. It was so very beautiful a Mass, and I was glad, for I had told Bill of my problem, and while they were all so busy and happy at the breakfast which fol-lowed the Mass, I slipped quietly away, to keep an appointment with a doctor.

He, too, recommended my immediate admis-sion to the hospital, and since I had already put the matter off for so long, I asked him if I could possibly wait until after the following Sunday, for on that day my beloved little Mary was beginning her long years of preparation for her life in God's service — she was entering Convent Station. He agreed, and that Sunday was one of the happiest I've known. What a privilege to be Mary's mother, and how grateful I am for such a blessing!

The following morning, I entered St. Francis Hospital here in Jersey City. I won't go into all the gruesome details of all the tests I underwent, but I'll never forget the moment of shocked disbelief when the doctor came to give me the result of the tests. I did not have a brain tumor, but I did have acute chorio-retinitis — I am going to be blind. No one could understand why I wasn't gleeful with joy at not having a brain tumor. They could not understand that in those first stunned moments it would have been much easier for me to face death instead of blindness. But there were three specialists who checked the tests, and I could not question their decision. Later that evening, I was talking to Father Rinfret on the phone. "Oh, pray for me, Father," I implored. "I am so ashamed of the poor, weak, mortal love that makes it so difficult for me to accept this new cross. I was perfectly willing to die; I was even happy in the thought, but the thought of being blind horrifies me."

"God would not have asked this of you, Mary," he said, if He were not absolutely sure that you had the courage to accept it. I'll be praying for you, and remembering you especially at Mass each day."

A few days later I wrote to him from the hospital, "You *must* be praying for me," I told him, "for I am learning to wear my crown of thorns with better grace. I can tell you now, in utter sincerity, that I want for myself only what God wants." During the days in the hospital, I looked back to the wonderful blind people on our pilgrimage, especially Sister Claire Cordis, and the thought of them and their ability to accept God's will so cheerfully brought me great consolation. And during the time I lay in my hospital bed, I was able to understand that the future, even without sight, need be no less blessed than the past. With my wonderful family and all the friends who volunteer to help with everything I've ever attempted (I do all the dreaming and they do all the work!) I knew I could go right on with our First Saturday Masses — yes, even with our pilgrimage plans for next year, with God's help.

Just before leaving the hospital, the doctor told me that these crazy headaches will last as long as sight does. When my sight burns out, so will the headaches, therefore even in so bleak a prospect there is some compensation. And even now, I am rushing to do as much of the pilgrimage work for next year as I can, while I can still see.

When my son, Jim, learned what the doctors had decided, he wrote to a friend of his, Brother Peter Thomas. The answer when it came was so touching that I've asked Jim's permission to quote it in part. After an assurance of prayers, the letter went on to say, "Your mom is a woman of deep and unshakable faith, Jim, and I am sure she will take this additional cross with the submission of Christ and the courage of Mary." I am not worthy of those words, Brother Peter, but in the days ahead, as the darkness closes in, I'll try to be!

\* \* \*

St. Mary's Lake at Our Lady of the Cape, with rosaries, the Sacred Heart and "VARICK" in lights.